GOLDENBALLS AND THE IRON LADY

A LITTLE BOOK OF NICKNAMES

GOLDENBALLS
AND **THE IRON LADY**

A LITTLE BOOK OF NICKNAMES

Andrew Delahunty

OXFORD
UNIVERSITY PRESS

OXFORD

UNIVERSITY PRESS

Great Clarendon Street, Oxford OX2 6DP

Oxford University Press is a department of the University of Oxford.
It furthers the University's objective of excellence in research, scholarship,
and education by publishing worldwide in

Oxford New York

Auckland Bangkok Buenos Aires Cape Town Chennai
Dar es Salaam Delhi Hong Kong Istanbul Karachi Kolkata Kuala Lumpur
Madrid Melbourne Mexico City Mumbai Nairobi
São Paulo Shanghai Taipei Tokyo Toronto

Oxford is a registered trade mark of Oxford University Press
in the UK and in certain other countries

Published in the United States
by Oxford University Press Inc., New York

British Library Cataloguing in Publication Data
Data available

Library of Congress Cataloging in Publication Data
Data available
ISBN 0-19-860964-7

1

Designed by Jane Stevenson
Typeset in Charter, Tekton, and Argo
by Footnote Graphics Ltd.
Printed in Great Britain
by Clays Ltd.
Bungay, Suffolk

Contents

List of Illustrations

Introduction

On 29 October 2003, the day that Iain Duncan Smith, the then leader of the UK Conservative Party, was expected to lose a vote of confidence among his party's MPs and be removed as leader, *The Sun* newspaper carried the headline 'Adios IDS'. The following morning's *Daily Mirror* headline was 'Dracula Stakes his Claim', referring to the fact that Michael Howard had declared himself a candidate for the leadership. Each of these headlines incorporates a nickname. Duncan Smith's long name was abbreviated to **IDS**, from his initials, while Howard owed his nickname **Dracula** to his slightly sinister image, underlined by his fellow MP Ann Widdecombe famously once saying that he had 'something of the night about him'. So, apart from helping journalists to produce pithy headlines, why do we give people nicknames?

Nicknames tell us something about the person nicknamed. Some are purely descriptive, drawing attention to some physical characteristic. Others highlight some personal quality or attribute or pay tribute to an achievement. A nickname often neatly sums someone up, providing an instant shorthand biography. In some ways an apt nickname resembles a cartoon or caricature. Indeed some nicknames such as **Supermac** (Harold Macmillan) and the **Iron Lady** (Margaret Thatcher) are closely tied up with how the people to whom they refer were represented by newspaper cartoonists. While many nicknames are clearly affectionate or admiring, many others express ridicule, contempt, or real hostility. Giving, say, a politician a nickname closes the gap between them and us, and can be a way of poking a little fun at our public figures and cutting them down to size. Nicknames have a habit of sticking to someone like a limpet and can have a damaging effect on someone's reputation, reinforcing unfavourable images, often by mockery. For example, such nicknames as **Wacko Jacko** (Michael Jackson), **Slick Willy** (Bill Clinton), and **Two Jags** (John Prescott) have dogged the people to whom they are attached.

This dictionary aims to identify and explain the origins of a wide range of nicknames applied to individual sports people, actors, musicians, politicians, and so on, concentrating on the 20th and 21st centuries. Although the bulk of the entries in this book explain the nicknames of individual people, you will also find included more generic nicknames such as **Ginger**, **Tiny**, and **Spike**. Some surnames invite the prefix of a certain nickname, like **Dusty** Miller and **Nobby** Clark. Such 'surname' nicknames are covered in these pages. Nicknames for countries, cities, US states, football clubs, and other places and organizations are also included. In addition to entries for individual nicknames, this book also features special boxed panels dealing with general themes: nicknames associated, for example, with boxers or jazz musicians, or thinness. There are also a number of panels devoted to people who have acquired multiple nicknames, such as Margaret Thatcher and Frank Sinatra.

What makes a good nickname? Importantly, there should be a recognition factor. A nickname should identify some characteristic that strikes a popular chord. In addition, the most memorable nicknames, the ones that really catch on, tend to make use of wordplay, rhyming, or alliteration. Puns often work well. Many nicknames play on an individual's real name, such as the **Thorpedo** (Ian Thorpe), **Bathing Towel** (Lord Baden-Powell), and **Jessyenormous** (Jessye Norman). Other nicknames, especially common in sport, depend on the person's surname being added in order to complete a punning phrase: Steve **Tugga** Waugh, Martin **Chariots** Offiah, Miguel **Singing** Indurain. Some nicknames are slight alterations of a familiar phrase or title: **Attila the Hen** (Margaret Thatcher), the **Prince of Wails** (Johnnie Ray), the **Lizard of Oz** (Paul Keating).

Many of the catchiest nicknames make use of rhyming or alliteration. Rhymes include **Elvis the Pelvis** (Elvis Presley), the **Muscles from Brussels** (Jean-Claude Van Damme), the **Ragin'**

Cajun (James Carville), **Stormin' Norman** (Norman Schwarzkopf). Alliterative nicknames include **Dugout Doug** (Douglas MacArthur), **Eddie the Eagle** (Eddie Edwards), **Lucky Lindy** (Charles Lindbergh), and the **Sultan of Swat** (Babe Ruth).

There is often a sense of playfulness and verbal inventiveness in nicknaming. Think of a trait. Speed, say. Among the many nicknames related to this characteristic in the field of sport are: **Arkle** (Derek Randall), the **Cannonball Kid** (Roscoe Tanner), the **Flying Dutchwoman** (Fanny Blankers-Koen), the **Rawalpindi Express** (Shoaib Akhtar), the **Rocket** (Rod Laver), the **Scud** (Mark Philippoussis), **White Lightning** (Alberto Juantorena, Allan Donald), **Wottle the Throttle** (Dave Wottle), and **Yifter the Shifter** (Miruts Yifter).

One nickname will sometimes inspire another. Eric Moussambani, the hopeless Equatorial Guinean swimmer at the 2000 Sydney Olympic Games, was instantly nicknamed **Eric the Eel** in the media. This was a deliberate echo of **Eddie the Eagle**, Eddie Edwards, the similarly hopeless British ski-jumper at the 1988 Winter Olympics in Calgary. Likewise, the popularity in Britain of the nickname **Gazza** (for the footballer Paul Gascoigne) led to a spate of copycat nicknames such as **Hezza** (Michael Heseltine) and **Prezza** (John Prescott).

People can have similar nicknames for quite different reasons. Cricketer Phil Tufnell was called **Cat** because he liked taking naps, whereas goalkeeper Peter Bonetti was known as the **Cat** because of his cat-like agility. While American footballer William Perry's nickname the **Refrigerator** referred to his bulk and fridge-emptying appetite, it was Chris Evert's supposed frostiness on the tennis court that led the press to dub her **Miss Frigidaire**.

I would like to thank Judy Pearsall and Rachel De Wachter of OUP for guiding this book through to publication and the book's copyeditor Sheila Ferguson for her careful attention to the text.

ASD
March 2004

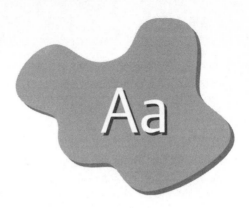

▶▶ Action Man

Before his marriage in 1981, Prince Charles (b.1948) was widely referred to as **Action Man** in the newspapers. The prince, who had served in the Royal Navy from 1971 to 1976, was frequently photographed pursuing a variety of adventurous and sporting activities, such as skiing, parachuting, windsurfing, deep-sea diving, and polo. Action Man is the tradename of a toy soldier figure.

▶▶ The Addicks

The origin of football team Charlton Athletic's nickname the **Addicks** has been much disputed. The word may simply be a corruption of *Athletic*. A more colourful theory, though, is that it derives from the word *haddock*, from a tradition that the fish used to be served as a supper to visiting teams.

▶▶ Afghan

The Australian cricketer Mark Waugh (b.1965) has one of the more ingenious nicknames in cricket. While his twin brother Steve first played for Australia in 1985–86, it wasn't until 1990–91 that Mark eventually made his Test debut, scoring 138 against England at Adelaide. The Australian press had taken to calling him **Afghan** (or **Afghanistan**), 'the forgotten Waugh'. This was a reference to 'the Forgotten War', that is, the Afghan War of the 1980s, when Soviet forces occupied Afghanistan. Waugh's other

nickname is **Junior**, since he is the younger twin. His
brother Steve's nickname ····➤ **TUGGA** is also a pun on their
surname.

➤➤ Air Jordan

Not only was **Air Jordan** the nickname of the US basketball
player Michael Jordan (b.1963), it was also the brand name
of a Nike sports shoe which he endorsed. His jumping ability
sometimes seemed to defy gravity. He was also known as **His
Airness**.

➤➤ Alligator Alley

Alligator Alley is the west–east section of the Tamiami Trail
(US 41) in the US state of Florida, running from Tampa to
Miami. It is crawling with alligators.

➤➤ All Souls' Parish Magazine

The Times newspaper was known as **All Souls' Parish
Magazine** during the 1920s and 30s, because the editor
G. G. Dawson, a fellow of All Souls College, Oxford, and
some of his associates, also fellows of the college, would
often meet there to discuss editorial policy.

➤➤ Ally Pally

Alexandra Palace, in Muswell Hill, North London, was used
from 1936 on as the first headquarters of BBC television. Its
affectionate nickname **Ally Pally** dates from around this time.
Originally designed as an exhibition centre, it was built in
1873.

➤➤ The Aloha State

The **Aloha State** is Hawaii. In Hawaiian *Aloha* means
'love' and is used when greeting or parting from
someone.

›› The Ambling Alp

The Italian boxer Primo Carnera (1906–67) was massive, a man-mountain at 6ft 5¾ins (197cm) tall and weighing 260lb (118kg). Carnera rose from circus strongman to world heavyweight champion 1933–34. Usually nicknamed the **Ambling Alp**, he was also known as the **Italian Alp** and **Da Preem**. He later gave up boxing to become a professional wrestler.

›› The American Caesar

During the Second World War, Douglas MacArthur (1880–1964) was in command of the US forces in the Far East and subsequently of the Allied Forces in the SW Pacific. He was later put in charge of UN military forces during the Korean War but clashed with President Truman, who relieved him of his command in 1951. MacArthur's reputation as a military commander led his admirers to call him the **American Caesar**.

›› The American Workhouse

London taxi drivers used to call the Park Lane Hotel the **American Workhouse**, an ironic reference to the palatial luxury enjoyed by rich American tourists staying there. The term dates from the early 20th century.

›› America's Boyfriend

The US film star Charles 'Buddy' Rogers (1904–99) was a matinee idol in the 1920s and was known as **America's Boyfriend**. It must have seemed the perfect match when in 1937 he married the actress Mary Pickford, known as **America's Sweetheart**.

›› America's Sweetheart

Mary Pickford (1893–1979) was one of the first stars of silent films, usually playing the innocent but plucky young heroine in such films as *Rebecca of Sunnybrook Farm* (1917), *Pollyanna* (1920), and *Tess of the Storm Country* (1932). For two decades the Canadian-born actress was the most popular screen star in the world, dubbed **America's Sweetheart** and later the **World's Sweetheart**. In 1919 she co-founded the film production company United Artists with Charlie Chaplin, D. W. Griffith, and her then husband Douglas Fairbanks. An astute businesswoman, she became one of America's richest women. The producer Sam Goldwyn once said: 'It took longer to make one of Mary's contracts than it did to make one of Mary's pictures'.

>> The Anatomic Bomb

Silvana Pampanini (b.1927), a former Miss Italy, was a voluptuous Italian film actress and sex-symbol of the 1950s. She was billed as the **Anatomic Bomb**, a fusion of *anatomy* and *atomic bomb*. The term had previously been used by MGM to promote an unknown Hollywood starlet called Linda Christian, in the summer of 1945, when the US had just dropped the first atomic bomb on Hiroshima.

>> The Angel of Death

Josef Mengele (1911–79) was a Nazi doctor who worked at the Auschwitz concentration camp (1943–45). He was known as the **Angel of Death** because of the barbaric 'medical experiments' he conducted and the power he wielded over life and death. It is thought that he was responsible for the deaths of 400,000 people.

>> The Animated Meringue

Barbara Cartland (1901–2000) was a prolific author of light romantic fiction. She was known for wearing full, pink chiffon dresses and heavy make-up, earning the nickname the **Animated Meringue** from the journalist Arthur Marshall.

❯❯ The Answer

Allen Iverson (b.1975), a basketball star with the
Philadelphia 76ers since 1996, is nicknamed the **Answer**
because his scoring ability is deemed to provide the answer
to any problem his team faces. Iverson has a multi-million
dollar sports shoe contract with Reebok and his nickname is
used on a line of basketball shoe. In 2003 a former friend
Jamil Blackmon filed a lawsuit claiming that he had coined
the nickname and that Iverson had promised him a
percentage of any merchandising royalties arising from its
use. The lawsuit was subsequently dismissed.

❯❯ The Apache State

The **Apache State** is one of the nicknames given to the US
state of Arizona. The Apache are an American Indian people
living chiefly in Arizona and New Mexico.

❯❯ Apple Isle

Australians sometimes refer to Tasmania as **Apple Isle** or
Apple Island, because it is noted as an apple-growing region.

❯❯ Arkle

The English cricketer Derek Randall (b.1951) was an
outstanding fielder, noted for the speed with which he
covered the ground and the accuracy of his throwing. His
Nottinghamshire teammates called him **Arkle**, after the
famous racehorse, winner of the Cheltenham Gold Cup three
years in a row (1964–66).

❯❯ A-Rod

The original **A-Rod** was the US baseball player Alex
Rodriguez (b.1975), who has played for the Seattle Mariners,
with whom he became one of the youngest players ever to
play in the major leagues, and the Texas Rangers. In 2003

Rodriguez became the youngest ever player to hit 300 home
runs. The nickname has also been applied to the US tennis
player Andy Roddick (b.1982), who ended 2003 as the world
no.1. Roddick won his first Grand Slam title in 2003, the US
Open. In 2004 he set the all-time record for the fastest serve
at 153mph.

›› The Athens of America

In the 19th century the US city of Boston gained the title the
Athens of America because of its blossoming as a centre of
cultural, literary, and educational activity. Boston's cultural
institutions include the Museum of Fine Arts, the Symphony
Orchestra, the Public Library, and the Athenaeum. Its
educational institutions include Boston University and
Harvard Medical School. The Greek city of Athens was an
important cultural centre in the 5th century BC.

›› The Athens of the North

Edinburgh was a flourishing cultural centre in the 18th and
19th centuries. The Scottish city was nicknamed the **Athens
of the North** because of its academic and intellectual
traditions, and the predominantly neoclassical style of
architecture in its city centre. Prominent Edinburgh-based
intellectual and literary figures included, David Hume, Adam
Smith, Robert Burns, Walter Scott, and Thomas Carlyle.

›› Attila the Hen

One of Margaret Thatcher's more amusing nicknames was
Attila the Hen. It is, of course, a pun on Attila the Hun
(406–53) and alludes both to Thatcher's authoritarian style
of leadership and her gender.

›› The Audi Chancellor

Gerhard Schröder (b.1944), the German Chancellor since
1998, has been dubbed the **Audi Chancellor** in Germany

because he has been married four times. His four (wedding) rings match the four-ring logo of the German car manufacturer.

›› The Auk

Claude Auchinleck (1884–1981) commanded the Allied forces in the First Battle of El Alamein in 1942 and the following year became Commander-in-Chief in India. He was made a field marshal in 1946. Auchinleck was universally known as the **Auk**, an army nickname that he had picked up before the war. Suggesting the name of the seabird, it is based on his surname.

›› Auld Reekie

Auld Reekie, literally 'Old Smoky', is Edinburgh. Dating back to the late 18th century, the nickname originally applied only to the old-town part of Edinburgh, but later came to refer to the whole city. It describes the smoky atmosphere produced by the city's many chimneys and thus corresponds to other big-city nicknames such as the **Smoke** and the **Big Smoke**.

›› Auntie

The BBC (British Broadcasting Corporation) has been known as **Auntie** since the arrival of British commercial television in the 1950s. The nickname initially reflected the BBC's image as a slightly prim, staid, and cosy institution in comparison with its brash new rival. The broadcaster is also known as ····➤ The BEEB.

›› Austerity Cripps

Stafford Cripps (1889–1952) served as Chancellor of the Exchequer 1947–50. As Chancellor, he presided over Britain's postwar austerity programme, involving such measures as rationing and voluntary wage freezes. Together with his rather puritanical demeanour, this is why he came to be known as **Austerity Cripps**.

1. Auntie

⟩⟩ The Austrian Oak

The **Austrian Oak** is the Austrian-born US film actor Arnold
Schwarzenegger (b.1947). His oak-like qualities are said to
lie not only in his muscular physique but also in his alleged
woodenness as an actor. A former bodybuilder and Mr
Universe, Schwarzenegger became a huge star of the 1980s
and 90s in such action films as *Terminator* (1984), *Total
Recall* (1990), *Terminator 2* (1991), and *True Lies* (1994).

⟩⟩ The Auto State

In the US, the **Auto State** is Michigan, the state where the city
of Detroit, home of the US automobile industry, is situated.

⟩⟩ The Aztec State

Arizona is called the **Aztec State** because the remains of old
Indian cultures were once believed to have been built by the
Aztecs.

>> Babe

Oliver Hardy (1892–1957) was the rotund half of the film
comedy partnership Laurel and Hardy. His nickname **Babe**
dates from early on in his career when he worked for the
Florida-based Lubin studio. According to his own account, he
used to get his hair cut by a local Italian barber: 'Well, he
took a great fancy to me and every time after he'd finish
shaving me, he'd rub powder into my face and pat my cheeks
and say, "Nice-a bab-ee, Nice-a bab-ee"'. His friends teased
him about this and started to call him **Baby**, later shortened
to **Babe**.

>> The Babe

Babe Ruth (1895–1948) is often regarded as the greatest
baseball player of all time. He was born George Herman Ruth
but was known as **Babe** from the age of 19, when he was
signed to the Baltimore Orioles by manager and owner Jack
Dunn and referred to as 'Jack's newest babe' by his
teammates. He later played for the Boston Red Sox
(1914–19) and the New York Yankees (1919–35). A
prodigious hitter, he set a record of 714 home runs which
remained unbroken until 1974.

>> Baby Doc

On the death in 1971 of François Duvalier (known as **Papa
Doc**), his son Jean-Claude Duvalier (b.1951) succeeded him

as President of Haiti at the age of 19. Jean-Claude's inevitable nickname was **Baby Doc**. He presided over a slightly more enlightened regime than his father but still refused to tolerate any political opposition. In 1986 a mass uprising forced Jean-Claude to flee the country.

›› The Baby-faced Assassin

The **Baby-faced Assassin** is a tag that has frequently been applied by journalists to a number of youthful-looking sportsmen. It is most closely associated with the footballer Ole Gunnar Solskjaer (b.1973), of Manchester United and Norway, and the Mexican boxer Marco Antonio Barrera (b.1974).

›› Baby Face Nelson

The US bank robber and gangland killer **Baby Face Nelson** (1908–34) was actually born Lester Nelson Gillis. Although he adopted the name George Nelson, his youthful looks, belying his violent personality, gave rise to his nickname, which he intensely disliked. He was killed in a shoot-out with FBI agents in 1934. A gangster with a similar nickname was ····➤ PRETTY Boy Floyd.

›› Backbone

The term **Backbone of...** is used to denote several ranges of mountains or hills. The Backbone of England is the Pennines, a range of hills in northern England, extending approximately 240 km (150 miles) from the Cheviot Hills near the Scottish border southwards to the Peak District in Derbyshire. The Backbone of Italy is the Apennines, a mountain range running 1,400 km (880 miles) down the entire length of Italy, from the north-west to the southern tip of the peninsula. The Backbone of North America is the Rocky Mountains (or Rockies), the chief mountain system of North America, extending more than 4,800 km (3,000 miles) from the US–Mexico border to the Yukon Territory of northern Canada. It separates the Great Plains from the Pacific coast and forms the Continental Divide.

❯❯ The Badger State

Inhabitants of the US state of Wisconsin are known as Badgers, perhaps because early 19th-century lead miners lived in caves in the hillside that were thought to resemble badger burrows. Wisconsin's nickname is thus the **Badger State** and the badger is its official state animal.

❯❯ The Baggies

West Bromwich Albion football club are known as the **Baggies**. This curious nickname is thought to derive not from the baggy shorts the team used to wear but from the loose-fitting working clothes worn by supporters coming straight from their shift at the local ironworks in the club's early days. Another possible explanation is that it referred to the men who used to carry the gate money in large cloth bags.

❯❯ Baillie Vass

Alec Douglas-Home (1903–95), Prime Minister 1963–64, was dubbed **Baillie Vass** (or the **Baillie**) by the satirical magazine *Private Eye*, after the *Aberdeen Evening Express* had printed photographs of the prime minister and a local official with the picture captions transposed. The magazine ironically pledged its support for the Conservatives with the slogan 'The Baillie will no' fail ye!'

❯❯ The Bald Eagle

The football manager Jim Smith (b.1940) is affectionately known as the **Bald Eagle** because of his lack of hair. He has managed a succession of clubs including Oxford United, Queen's Park Rangers, Newcastle United, and Derby County.

⟫ Baldilocks

Gerald Kaufman (b.1930), the British Labour politician, was nicknamed **Baldilocks** by the satirical magazine *Private Eye*. It is, of course, a mocking variation on Goldilocks, and draws attention to the politician's baldness.

⟫ Bambi

Some nicknames are quite short-lived. When Tony Blair (b.1953) became leader of the Labour Party in 1994, his relative youth and inexperience led the British press initially to give him the nickname **Bambi**, after the young deer in Felix Salten's children's story and the Disney film. Cartoonists attempted to depict Blair as Bambi, but the nickname didn't really catch on. Blair was soon being criticized for an authoritarian style of leadership, causing him to remark at a party conference: 'Hard for me sometimes. 1994, Bambi; 1995, Stalin. From Disneyland to dictatorship in 12 short months. I'm not sure which one I prefer. OK, I prefer Bambi. Honestly.'

2. *Tony Blair as Bambi, June 1994*

❯❯ The Bambino

Babe Ruth (1895–1948) was sometimes known as the
Bambino, particularly by Italian-American baseball fans. This
was the Italian version of ⋯➤ the **BABE**.

❯❯ Barnacle

The English cricketer Trevor Bailey (b.1923) was an
outstanding all-rounder of the 1950s and a master of
defensive batting. His tenacious refusal as a batsman to be
removed from the crease, no matter how slowly he was
scoring runs, earned him the nickname **Barnacle**.

❯❯ Bart's

Bart's is the familiar name for St Bartholomew's Hospital,
the oldest hospital in London on its original site (founded in
1123). Its famous medical college was founded in 1662.

❯❯ Bathing Towel

Robert Baden-Powell (1857–1941), 1st Baron Baden-Powell,
founded the Boy Scout movement (later called the Scout
Association) in 1908. His nickname **Bathing Towel**, playing
on his double-barrelled surname, can be traced back to his
Charterhouse schooldays.

❯❯ The Battle-born State

On 31 October 1864 Nevada was admitted to the Union, at
the height of the American Civil War, hence its nickname the
Battle-born State.

❯❯ The Bayou State

The US state of Mississippi has an abundance of bayous
(marshy outlets of lakes or rivers), from which it derives its
nickname the **Bayou State**.

>> The Bay State

Massachusetts is sometimes called the **Bay State**, a reference
to the early colony of Massachusetts Bay. After the Pilgrim
Fathers founded Plymouth Colony in Massachusetts in 1620,
another settlement, Massachusetts Bay Colony, was founded
in Salem in 1628.

>> Bean

Coleman Hawkins (1904–69), the US jazz saxophonist,
played with the Fletcher Henderson band in the 1920s and
1930s and his huge-toned sound helped to establish the
tenor saxophone as a jazz instrument. Although he came to
be more generally known as **Hawk**, he was earlier given the
nickname **Bean**, apparently in reference to his alleged
meanness, as justified by his frequent remark 'I haven't a
bean'. It has also been suggested that the name conveys the
idea of Hawkins as a fertile source of musical creativity.

>> The Bear

The US general H. Norman Schwarzkopf (b.1935) was
sometimes known in the army before the Gulf War as the
Bear. He was thought to be bear-like in his size and his
volatile temper. Schwarzkopf became better known as
····▶ **STORMIN'** Norman.

>> The Beard

Monty Woolley (1888–1963) was a former Yale professor
who became a film star in his fifties with his performance as
the sharp-tongued wit and radio celebrity Sheridan
Whiteside in *The Man Who Came to Dinner* (1941). He was
known as the **Beard** because of his trademark professorial
beard.

≫ The Beast of ...

The **Beast of Belsen** was Josef Kramer (1906–45), the
notoriously cruel German commandant of the Belsen
concentration camp from December 1944. At the end of the
Second World War he was tried before a British military
tribunal and executed in November 1945. The **Beast of
Buchenwald** (or the **Bitch of Buchenwald**) was Ilse Koch
(d.1967), the wife of the commandant of the Nazi
concentration camp at Buchenwald, in eastern Germany. She
became infamous for the atrocities she committed there.

≫ The Beast of Bolsover

The Labour politician Dennis Skinner (b.1932) has been MP
for Bolsover in Derbyshire since 1970. Famous for his
forthright left-wing views and abrasive manner, he has a
reputation for heckling other MPs and interrupting their
speeches. His long-standing nickname the **Beast of Bolsover**
was originally applied to Skinner by parliamentary
correspondents.

≫ Beast 666

Aleister Crowley (1875–1947) was a British occultist and
mystic who became notorious for practising black magic and
for his sexual immorality. Crowley identified himself with the
Beast from the Book of Revelation, whose name is said to be
numerologically represented by the number 666: 'Let him
that hath understanding count the number of the beast: for it
is the number of a man; and his number is Six hundred
threescore and six' (Revelation 13:18). As well as **Beast 666**
Crowley revelled in the title the British tabloids gave him: the
Wickedest Man in the World.

≫ The Beaver

William Maxwell Aitken, Lord Beaverbrook (1879–1964),
was the Canadian-born newspaper magnate who owned the

British newspaper the *Daily Express*. He was known to his staff as the **Beaver**, partly from his title (itself taken from the New Brunswick town in Canada where he had a home) and partly from his beaver-like industriousness.

›› The Beaver State

In the US, the **Beaver State** is Oregon. The nickname reflects the widespread identification between the timber-producing state and the tree-gnawing rodent, the official state animal.

›› Beckingham Palace

Beckingham Palace is a humorous newspaper nickname for the home of David and Victoria Beckham, a £2.5 million neo-Georgian mansion in Sawbridgeworth, Hertfordshire noted for its extravagance. The nickname is a blend of their surname and *Buckingham Palace*, the London residence of the British sovereign.

›› Becks

Many footballers' nicknames are simply abbreviations of their surnames. The most famous example currently is **Becks**, David Beckham (b.1975). He has played for Manchester United, Real Madrid, and England, having been appointed captain of the national team in 2000. Outside the world of football, Beckham is famous as one half of the celebrity couple **Posh and Becks**. He is married to Victoria Adams, formerly known as Posh Spice in the pop group the Spice Girls.

›› The Beeb

The term **Beeb**, referring to the BBC, dates from the 1960s and derives from the first part of the initials BBC, spoken aloud. The broadcaster is also known as ····▶ AUNTIE.

» Beefy

In cricket, **Beefy** was the powerfully-built English all-rounder Ian Botham (b.1955). He was the first player to complete a Test double of over 5,000 runs and 300 wickets. In 1978 Botham became the first player to score 100 runs and take 8 wickets in one innings of a Test match.

» The Beehive State

The **Beehive State** is Utah. A conical beehive, surrounded by a swarm of bees, appears on the state flag. This is meant to symbolize the industriousness of the Mormon inhabitants of Utah. The first Mormon settlers named the state Deseret (meaning 'honeybee').

» Bertie

Queen Victoria called her son Edward (later to be Edward VII) **Bertie**. He was christened Albert Edward after his father.

» The Bhoys

Celtic football club are known as the **Bhoys**. The Glasgow club was formed from a group of Catholic Boys' Club sides and the unusual spelling of the word was probably intended to represent the Irish pronunciation.

» The Bible Belt

The term the **Bible Belt** refers to those areas of the southern and middle western United States and western Canada where Protestant fundamentalism is widely practised. It comes from the abundance of itinerant Bible salesmen in the region and was coined by H. L. Mencken, about 1925.

» The Big Apple

Why New York City is known as the **Big Apple** is something of a mystery. The phrase seems to have been first used in the

1920s, perhaps after the name of a Harlem night club used by jazz musicians, which became synonymous with the city itself. Another possible explanation is that the Spanish word for a block of buildings is *manzana*, which is also the word for an apple. Or the expression may refer to the apple in the Garden of Eden, characterizing the city as a den of temptation and sin. Whatever its origin, the term was revived in the 1970s as part of a publicity campaign designed to improve the city's image, with the slogan 'New York City — the Big Apple'.

›› Big Bill[1]

William Hale Thompson (1867–1944) was the mayor of Chicago three times 1915–23. Known as **Big Bill**, or sometimes as **Bill the Builder**, Thompson was responsible for a major building and construction programme in the city. Less admirably, under his tenure Chicago also picked up a reputation for corruption, gangsterism, and lawlessness. The nickname Big Bill is also sometimes applied to William Howard Taft (1857–1930), the 27th President of the US (1909–13).

›› Big Bill[2]

Bill Tilden (1893–1953) dominated tennis in the 1920s, winning Wimbledon three times (1920–21, 1930) and the US Open seven times (1920–25, 1929). A tall man of 6ft 2ins (188cm), he was known as **Big Bill**, partly to distinguish him from his great rival Bill Johnston (1894–1946), 5ft 8½ ins (174cm) tall and accordingly known as **Little Bill**.

›› Big Bird

The West Indian fast bowler Joel Garner (b.1952) was, at 6ft 8ins (203cm), one of the tallest Test cricketers ever. His long arms meant that the ball would be hurtling towards the batsman from well over 8ft. His nickname **Big Bird** was borrowed from the character of the same name, an enormous yellow bird, in the US children's TV programme *Sesame Street*.

❯❯ Big Blue

The computer company IBM (in full International Business Machines) was known as **Big Blue** at the time of its market dominance, from its blue and white logo and the blue covers on much of its early hardware.

❯❯ Big Cat

Clive Lloyd (b.1944), the West Indian cricketer, was known as **Big Cat** (or **Big C** or **Supercat**) because of the lightning speed of his fielding and explosive power of his batting, both belied by his relaxed manner and loping walk. Lloyd played in 110 Test matches, captaining the West Indies in 74 of them. He scored 19 Test centuries, including ones in his debuts against both England and Australia.

❯❯ Big Daddy

Idi Amin (full name Idi Amin Dada) (1925–2003) was Uganda's head of state 1971–79. His regime was notorious for its brutality and repression, during which Uganda's Asian population was expelled and thousands of his political opponents murdered. He gave himself the nickname **Big Daddy**. Amin was overthrown in 1979 and forced to flee the country.

❯❯ The Big Easy[1]

The US city of New Orleans is known as the **Big Easy**, from the relaxed pace of life there. In the early 1900s this was the name of a New Orleans dance hall and the term subsequently transferred to the city itself.

❯❯ The Big Easy[2]

Ernie Els (b.1969), the South African golfer, gets his nickname the **Big Easy** from his 6ft 3ins (190cm) frame, his natural, apparently effortless swing, and his easy-going manner. Els won the US Open in 1994 and 1997 and the British Open in 2002. He took three successive World Match Play titles 1994–96.

>> The Big Fellow

As a member of Parliament for Sinn Fein, Michael Collins (1890–1922), was one of the negotiators of the Anglo-Irish Treaty of 1921. He commanded the Irish Free State forces in the civil war and became head of state but was assassinated ten days later. Collins, a powerfully built man, was affectionately known as the **Big Fellow** by his supporters.

>> Big-Hearted Arthur

The ever-cheerful comedian Arthur Askey (1900–82) applied the nickname **Big-Hearted Arthur** to himself in the first edition of his radio show *Band Waggon* in 1938. From then on the label was used as part of his billing.

>> Big Jack

Big Jack is Jack Charlton (b.1935), the English footballer and manager. A robust defender, he played for Leeds United (1952–73) and England. Charlton managed a number of league clubs before becoming manager of the Republic of Ireland national team (1986–95), whom he took to the quarter-finals of the World Cup in 1990. In his playing days he was also known as the **Giraffe** because of his long neck.

>> Big Mac

As well as being the well-known brand name of a hamburger, **Big Mac** is Mark McGwire (b.1963), the US baseball player. In 1998, playing for the St Louis Cardinals, he hit 70 home runs in the season, setting a new record. His great rival Sammy Sosa hit 66 home runs for the Chicago Cubs in the same season.

►► Big O

The US singer Roy Orbison (1936–88), otherwise known as
the **Big O**, shot to fame with the ballad 'Only the Lonely'
(1960). His subsequent hits include 'Crying' (1961) and 'Oh,
Pretty Woman' (1964), one of the best-selling singles of the
1960s. Another nickname where O stands for a surname is
····► JACKIE O.

►► Big Ron

Ron Atkinson (b.1939) is in some ways the stereotype of the
football manager. Known for his extrovert and flashy image,
Atkinson has managed many clubs including West Bromwich
Albion, Atlético Madrid, Manchester United, Sheffield
Wednesday, and Aston Villa. Many other football managers
have picked up the **Big** tag, including **Big Mal**, Malcolm
Allison (b.1927) and **Big Joe**, Joe Royle (b.1949).

►► The Big Ship

The Australian cricketer Warwick Windridge Armstrong
(1879–1947) captained Australia in the 1920s, leading his
team to eight successive wins against England (1920–21). An
accomplished all-rounder, Armstrong weighed 22 stone
(140kg) at the end of his career, hence his nickname the
Big Ship.

►► Big Sky

Joe Montana (b.1956) was one of American football's
greatest quarterbacks. He played for the San Francisco 49ers
in four of the team's winning Super Bowls (1982, 1985,
1989, 1990). He was inevitably known as **Big Sky** since one
of the nicknames of the US state of Montana is the **Big Sky
State**. Another of his nicknames was **Cool Joe**.

►► The Big Smoke

Before clean-air legislation, large cities were known for the

smoky, sooty atmosphere produced by their many chimneys.
In Britain the terms the **Smoke** or the **Big Smoke** are usually
applied to London. In Australia, the terms can refer to any
large city or town, but chiefly to Sydney or Melbourne.
Edinburgh is known as ····➤ AULD Reekie for a similar reason.

➤➤ Big T

Jack Teagarden (1905–64), the US jazz trombonist and
bandleader, was known as **Big T**. The T stood not only for
Teagarden but also for Texas, where he was born. His
younger brother Charles, who played the trumpet, was
known as **Little T**.

➤➤ Big Train

Walter Johnson (1887–1946) was one of the fastest pitchers
in the history of baseball. Early in his career, he was given
the name **Big Train** because of the speed of his deliveries
and his stature: 6ft 1in (1.85m) and 200lb (91kg). He
played the whole of his 21-year career for the Washington
Senators.

➤➤ The Big Yin

When performing stand-up in the 1980s, the Scottish
comedian and actor Billy Connolly (b.1942) was
affectionately known as the **Big Yin**, Scottish dialect for 'the
Big One'. The term was used by Connolly himself in one of
his routines to refer to Jesus Christ.

➤➤ The Biograph Girl

Florence Lawrence (1886–1938) was one of Hollywood's first
stars of silent films. In the days when screen actors were
largely anonymous, she became highly popular with
audiences and was promoted as the **Biograph Girl**. 'Biograph'
was an early term for a cinema. It was also the name of D. W.
Griffith's New York Studios (1903–10).

❯❯ Bird

Bird, one of the most famous nicknames in jazz, was Charlie
Parker (1920–55), the brilliant alto saxophonist who with the
trumpeter Dizzy Gillespie founded the bebop movement. The
nickname is itself an abbreviation of **Yardbird**, an earlier
nickname. There are several versions of the story of how
Parker came by his nickname, usually related to his fondness
for eating chicken. According to one account, in the early
1940s his band were driving to a gig in Lincoln, Nebraska
when one of their cars ran over a stray chicken in the road.
Parker was keen to pick up the 'yardbird' so that they could
cook it later for dinner. The name stuck and was later
shortened to Bird. In 1988 Clint Eastwood directed a film
biography of Parker with the title *Bird*.

❯❯ The Birdman of Alcatraz

Robert Stroud (1890–1963) served 54 years in prison for two
murders, 28 of them at the top-security prison Alcatraz in
San Francisco Bay, California. In his prison cell he turned
himself into a noted ornithologist, becoming known as the
Birdman of Alcatraz. A 1961 film of this title starred Burt
Lancaster as Stroud.

❯❯ The Birthplace of Aviation

The US city of Dayton, Ohio was the home of the US aviation
pioneers Wilbur (1867–1912) and Orville (1871–1948)
Wright. Dayton remains a centre of aerospace research.

❯❯ The Biscuitmen

Reading football club used to rejoice in the nickname the
Biscuitmen. This is because their ground Elm Park was at
one time owned by the biscuit manufacturer Huntley and
Palmer. When the company left Reading in 1974, a new
nickname the **Royals** was then adopted, though the old one
has not been forgotten by the fans.

❯❯ Biscuit Pants

Though better known as ⋯⋯➤ **IRON** Horse, the US baseball player Lou Gehrig (1903–41) was called **Biscuit Pants** by his teammates, because of his heavy build.

❯❯ The Bishop

Jess Yates (1918–93) is best known for presenting in the 1970s the long-running British TV programme *Stars on Sunday*, in which guests from the world of show business sang hymns and read passages from the Bible. Yates, a former cinema organist, was known as the **Bishop** because of the programme's religious content.

❯❯ Bites Yer Legs

One of the most fondly remembered footballing nicknames is **Bites Yer Legs**. This belonged to Norman Hunter (b.1943), a central defender with Leeds United and England in the 1960s and 1970s. Hunter's intimidating nickname came from his ferocious tackling.

❯❯ The Black Cats

The **Black Cats** is a rare example of a nickname being chosen by popular acclaim. When in 1997 Sunderland football club moved from its Roker Park stadium to the Stadium of Light, the club decided to replace its former nickname the **Rokerites** (or **Rokermen**) with a new one. In 2000, following a poll of fans, the **Black Cats** was chosen, with 48% of the votes cast. The name refers to a battery of guns that was positioned at the mouth of the River Wear in the 18th century. The runner-up was the **Mackems** (a local word for inhabitants of Sunderland), with 37% of the votes.

❯❯ Black Jack

General John Pershing (1860–1948) was commander-in-chief of the American forces in Europe in the First World War. He subsequently gave his name to the Pershing missile, a type of short-range surface-to-surface ballistic missile. Before the war, Pershing commanded a black cavalry unit, hence his army nickname at the time, **Nigger Jack**. When he became better known, this was modified to the more generally acceptable **Black Jack**.

>> The Black Octopus

Lev Yashin (1929–91) was the goalkeeper of the Soviet Union's national football team between 1954 and 1967. His nickname was the **Black Octopus** (or sometimes the **Black Spider**) because he always wore an all-black strip and his astonishing agility and reflexes gave the impression that he had more than the usual number of limbs.

>> The Black Panther[1]

Donald Neilson (b.1936) was convicted in 1976 of kidnapping and murdering the teenage heiress Lesley Whittle and shooting dead three post office workers. He disguised himself by wearing a black hood, hence the press nickname the **Black Panther**.

>> The Black Panther[2]

The Mozambique-born Portuguese footballer Eusébio (Eusébio Ferreira da Silva) (b.1942) signed for the Lisbon club Benfica in 1961, going on to score 316 goals in 294 league appearances. Eusébio won 64 international caps for Portugal, scoring 41 goals. In the 1966 World Cup he was the top scorer with nine goals. He was known as the **Black Panther** and also as the **New Pelé**.

>> The Black Pearl

Many people regard the Brazilian footballer Pelé (born Edson Arantes do Nascimento) (b.1940) as the greatest player of all time. For most of his playing career his club side was Santos (1955–74). He made his debut for Brazil at the age of 17 and went on to appear for his country 111 times, scoring 97 goals. Pelé took part in four World Cup competitions, three of which Brazil won (1958, 1962, and 1970). Admired around the world, he was nicknamed the **Black Pearl**.

›› The Blades

Sheffield United football club are known as the **Blades**, from Sheffield's traditional steel industry, especially the making of cutlery. Surprisingly, this had originally been the nickname of United's great local rivals Sheffield Wednesday, before they adopted the nickname the **Owls**.

›› Blanco

Blanco is one of the traditional nicknames in the British armed forces for a man with the surname White. It comes from the brand name of a white preparation for whitening belts, webbing, and other pieces of equipment, used from the late 19th century until the 1960s. Another common nickname for someone called White is **Chalky**.

›› The Blessed Margaret

One of Margaret Thatcher's nicknames was the **Blessed Margaret**, coined by the Conservative politician Norman St John Stevas (b.1929), Leader of the House of Commons (1979–81).

›› Blighty

To soldiers serving abroad in the First and Second World Wars, **Blighty** was England or Britain, thought of as home. During the First World War, a wound which was serious enough for a soldier to be sent back home to Britain was itself known as a Blighty. The term originated among British soldiers serving in India, and is an Anglo-Indian alteration of

Urdu *bilā yatī* 'foreign, European', from Arabic *wilā yat*, *wilā ya* 'dominion, district'.

›› The Blonde Bombshell

Jean Harlow (1911–37) was a wisecracking platinum-blonde film star and sex-symbol of the 1930s. Her films include *Hell's Angels* (1930), *Red Dust* (1932), *Dinner at Eight* (1933), and *Bombshell* (1933). Although originally applied to Harlow, the term 'blonde bombshell' can be used to describe any startlingly attractive blonde woman.

›› Blood and Guts

George Patton (1885–1945) was the Second World War general who commanded the 7th Army during the Sicilian campaign (1943) and the 3rd Army in the Normandy invasion (1944), advancing rapidly across France and into Germany. His soldiers called him **Blood and Guts** or **Old Blood and Guts**, reflecting his unpredictable temper and his arrogant, outspoken, and dominant personality.

›› Bloody Balfour

Arthur Balfour (1848–1930), the Conservative Prime Minister 1902–5, earned the nickname **Bloody Balfour** after an incident when he was Irish Chief Secretary earlier in his career. In 1887, following the prosecution of the nationalist leader William O'Brien for conspiracy, two protesting rioters were shot and killed by police at Mitchelstown, County Cork. Irish nationalists vilified Balfour as **Bloody Balfour**.

›› Bluebeard

In a tale by Charles Perrault, the character of Bluebeard kills several wives in turn and keeps their remains in a locked room. The name was later attached to Henri Landru (1869–1922), a French murderer who killed ten women over a five-year period, having first proposed marriage to them. It has subsequently been applied to various murderous husbands or mass killers of women.

▶▶ The Bluebirds

The **Bluebirds** are Cardiff City football club, who play in a blue-and-white strip. The nickname dates back to 1911–12 when Maurice Maeterlinck's play *L'Oiseau Bleu* ('The Blue Bird') was performed in Cardiff.

▶▶ The Bluegrass State

Kentucky is known as the **Bluegrass State**. Bluegrass is a term for any grass with bluish flowers found abundantly in the central region of Kentucky. This grass provides rich pasture for horses and has led to the state becoming a centre of racehorse breeding in the US.

▶▶ The Blue Hen State

The inhabitants of Delaware are known as Blue Hen's Chickens. The term dates from the early 1800s and is said to have come from a company in the American War of Independence, led by a Captain Caldwell of Delaware. He owned two gamecocks, the offspring of a blue hen, that fought fiercely and courageously, just like his men. The company became known in Carolina as 'Caldwell's gamecocks', and later as 'the blue hen's chickens' and the 'blue chickens'. In turn, Delaware became known as the **Blue Hen State**.

▶▶ Bluey

Bluey is an Australian nickname for a red-haired man, dating from the end of the 19th century. This is one of those humorous invertions, on the lines of Tiny for a large person and Curly for a bald man. A bluey was also a bundle of possessions carried by a bushman, so called because its outer covering was traditionally a blue blanket.

❯❯ Bob de Bilde

Gilles de Bilde (b.1971) is a Belgian footballer who has
played for Anderlecht, Sheffield Wednesday, and Aston Villa.
When de Bilde played for Sheffield Wednesday, his
teammates called him **Bob**, a delightful pun on the British
children's TV character Bob the Builder.

❯❯ The Bod

In Oxford, the **Bod** is the informal name for the Bodleian
Library, the library of Oxford University. The first library was
established in the 14th century, but it was refounded by
Thomas Bodley (1545–1613), greatly expanded, and
renamed the Bodleian in 1604.

❯❯ The Body

The shapely figures of a number of famous women have
earned them the nickname the **Body**. Perhaps the first of
these was the film actress and ex-model Marie McDonald
(1923–65). The Australian model Elle MacPherson (b.1963)
developed her modelling career in the US, where she too
became known as the **Body**, a name that was also applied in
the 1980s to the Hollywood actress Jamie Lee Curtis
(b.1958).

❯❯ Bogie

Bogie, sometimes spelt **Bogey**, was Humphrey Bogart
(1899–1957), the US film actor. He made his name as a
gangster in *The Petrified Forest* (1936). In the 1940s and
1950s he appeared in the role of the tough, cynical, yet soft-
hearted hero in such films as *The Maltese Falcon* (1941),
Casablanca (1942), *The Big Sleep* (1946), and *The African
Queen* (1951).

➤➤ The Boil

The cricketer Trevor Bailey's (b.1923) nickname the **Boil**
derives from the apparent shouts of 'Come on, Boiley' from
Cockney spectators at a football match he was playing in.

➤➤ Bomber Harris

Arthur Harris (1892–1984), known as **Bomber** Harris, was
Commander-in-Chief of Bomber Command (1942–45) in the
Second World War. He organized mass bombing raids against
Dresden and other German cities which resulted in large-
scale civilian casualties. This strategy of heavy area bombing
proved to be controversial and badly affected Harris's
postwar reputation.

➤➤ Bones

In the late 1930s, before he became a solo star, Frank Sinatra
(1915–98) was a singer with Tommy Dorsey's band. The
other musicians used to call him **Bones** on account of his
skinny frame.

➤➤ Bonking Boris

At the age of 17, Boris Becker (b.1967), the German tennis
player, became the youngest man to win the men's singles
championship at Wimbledon in 1985, the first time that the
title had been won by an unseeded player. He retained the
Wimbledon title the following year, but in 1987 Becker lost
to the Australian Peter Doohan in the second round.
According to the British tabloids, his unexpected loss of form
was because he had been having too much sex and so they
dubbed him **Bonking Boris**.

➤➤ Bosie

It was Oscar Wilde's relationship with Lord Alfred Douglas
(1870–1945), affectionately known as **Bosie**, that ultimately
resulted in Wilde's imprisonment for homosexual offences.

Wilde's essay *De Profundis* (1905), written in Reading Gaol, is addressed to Douglas. **Bosie** comes from 'Boysie', which is what his mother used to call him.

▶▶ The Boss

Bruce Springsteen (b.1949), the US rock singer, songwriter, and guitarist, is widely known as the **Boss** by rock fans and journalists. Born in New Jersey, Springsteen writes songs about blue-collar life and is known for his energetic stage performances. Springsteen's nickname came about from his early days playing gigs in small venues with his backing band, the E-Street Band. At the end of each week it was his responsibility to collect the money and pay the rest of the band, and this led them to start calling him the Boss. 'I hate bosses', Springsteen has complained since, 'I hate being called the Boss.'

▶▶ The Boston Strangler

Between June 1962 and January 1964, Albert H. DeSalvo (1933–73) killed at least eleven elderly women in Boston, all of whom he strangled. The **Boston Strangler**, as the press called the killer, was later identified as DeSalvo, who had already been arrested for a large number of sexual assaults, for which he was given a life sentence in 1967. He was later stabbed to death in prison by one or more fellow inmates.

▶▶ The Bouncing Czech

Robert Maxwell (1923–91), the Czech-born British publisher and media entrepreneur, built up a considerable publishing empire during the 1980s. After his mysterious death while yachting off Tenerife, it emerged that he had misappropriated the pension funds of some of his companies. He was known by the British tabloids as the **Bouncing Czech**, a pun inspired by his ability to bounce back from a number of financial scandals. Another nickname was **Captain Bob**.

Boxers

Most boxers' ring names follow a well-established formula. Many are alliterative:

Ambling Alp — Primo Carnera
Brown Bomber — Joe Louis
Dancing Destroyer — Herbie Hide
Homicide Hank — Henry Armstrong
Marvelous Marvin — Marvin Hagler

There is a long tradition of such alliterative nicknames incorporating the name of the boxer's birthplace:

Boston Strong Boy — John L. Sullivan
Brockton Blockbuster — Rocky Marciano
Bronx Bull — Jake LaMotta
Clones Cyclone — Barry McGuigan
Detroit Destroyer — Joe Louis
Livermore Larruper — Max Baer
Louisville Lip — Muhammad Ali
Manassa Mauler — Jack Dempsey
Tonypandy Terror — Tommy Farr

Some of the most intimidating nicknames simply focus on the power and ferocity of the boxer's punches:

Bonecrusher — James Smith
Hit Man — Thomas Hearns
Iron Mike — Mike Tyson

›› Boy Bonkers

Jonny Wilkinson (b.1979) kicked the decisive drop goal that won the 2003 Rugby World Cup Final for England against Australia. His nickname **Boy Bonkers** stems from his intense

demeanour on the pitch and press speculation during the
World Cup tournament that he was cracking under the strain
of media scrutiny and public expectation. Although normally
left-footed, Wilkinson kicked the winning drop goal with
his right foot, prompting *The Guardian*'s headline, 'Wrong
foot is right stuff for Boy Bonkers'. His teammates call him
Wilko.

›› Boycs

Geoffrey Boycott (b.1940) began his cricketing career with
Yorkshire in 1962 and first played for England two years
later. Boycott was an outstanding opening batsman and
prolific run-maker who had scored more than 150 centuries
by the time he retired from first-class cricket in 1986. He
scored 8,114 runs in Test cricket (1964–82). Although
usually referred to informally as **Boycs**, to his many admirers
at Yorkshire CC he was **Sir Geoffrey**.

›› The Boy David

David Steel (b.1938) led the Liberal Party 1976–88 and was
briefly joint leader with David Owen of the Social and Liberal
Democrats. At the age of 26, he was elected to parliament in
1965, becoming the youngest MP at the time. During the late
70s and 80s Steel was known as the **Boy David**, which
seemed to fit his youthful looks and his perceived role as the
junior partner both in the Lib–Lab pact, a temporary political
alliance with Labour (1977–78), and in his relationship with
David Owen. He served as speaker of the new Scottish
parliament 1999–2003.

›› The Boy Wonder

In 1930s' Hollywood, the **Boy Wonder** was Irving Thalberg
(1899–1936), the young film producer who was appointed
head of production at Universal Pictures at the age of 20,
then made head of the newly formed MGM studio at 25. He

produced such MGM films as *Grand Hotel* (1932), *The Barretts of Wimpole Street* (1934), and *Mutiny on the Bounty* (1935). The tag was also used for Robin, the young crime-fighting partner of the comic-book superhero Batman, and the term 'boy wonder' can be applied to any exceptionally talented young man or boy.

›› Brab

The British pioneer aviator and politician John Theodore Cuthbert Moore-Brabazon, 1st Baron Brabazon of Tara (1884–1964), had a name which was rather a mouthful, so he was popularly known as **Brab**. He was the first British citizen to hold a pilot's licence (1910) and served as Minister of Transport and Minister of Aircraft in the coalition government during the Second World War.

›› The Brazilian Bombshell

Although born in Portugal, Carmen Miranda (1909–55) lived in Brazil from childhood, hence her nickname when she later appeared in movies, the **Brazilian Bombshell**. She starred in such Hollywood musicals as *Down Argentina Way* (1940) and *The Gang's All Here* (1943). She had a flamboyant style and wore exotic costumes which often featured an elaborate hat or turban packed high with tropical fruit and flowers.

›› Brenda

Elizabeth II (b.1926), Queen of the United Kingdom since 1952, is known by the satirical magazine *Private Eye* as **Brenda**.

›› Brian

Brian is the nickname used in the satirical magazine *Private Eye* for Charles, Prince of Wales (b.1948).

❯❯ Broadway Joe

Joe Namath (b.1943), the American football player, played
for the New York Jets 1965–77, leading them to an upset
victory over the Baltimore Colts in the 1969 Super Bowl.
Namath's nickname **Broadway Joe** fitted his glamorous image
as a metropolitan playboy.

❯❯ The Brockton Blockbuster

Rocky Marciano (1923–69) became world heavyweight
boxing champion in 1952 and successfully defended his title
six times. After 49 professional fights as a heavyweight, he
retired undefeated in 1956. He was born Rocco Francis
Marchegiano and his nickname derives from his home town
of Brockton, Massachusetts, and the ferocity of his punching.

❯❯ The Bronx Bull

The boxer Jake LaMotta (b.1921) was the first man to beat
Sugar Ray Robinson (in 1943) and became world
middleweight champion in 1949. In the ring he would charge
with a low crouching stance, which, together with his
birthplace of the Bronx, New York, accounted for his
nickname the **Bronx Bull**. Robert De Niro played him in the
film *Raging Bull* (1980).

❯❯ The Brown Bomber

Joe Louis (1914–81) was heavyweight boxing champion of the
world for nearly 12 years (1937–49), defending his title 25
times during that period, a record for any weight. All but four
of these victories were knockouts, his devastating punching
earning him his famous nickname the **Brown Bomber**.

❯❯ The Brown Eminence

In 1941 Martin Bormann (1900–c.1945) succeeded Rudolf
Hess as Nazi Party chancellor. Considered to be Hitler's

closest collaborator, he disappeared at the end of the Second
World War but was nevertheless sentenced to death in his
absence at the Nuremberg trials in 1945. Persistent rumours
that he had escaped to Argentina were finally quelled in 1973
when his skeleton, exhumed in Berlin, was identified.
Bormann was known as the **Brown Eminence** in a conscious
echo of the **Grey Eminence**, as Cardinal Richelieu's influential
private secretary François Leclerc du Tremblay (1577–1638)
was called. The later nickname comes from the Brownshirts,
the Nazi storm troopers founded by Hitler in Munich in 1921,
whose brown uniforms resembled those of Mussolini's
Blackshirts.

❯❯ Brum

Brum, an informal name for the city of Birmingham, is a
shortened form of Brummagem, originally (in the mid 17th
century) a dialect form of the city's name. The term
Brummagem came to be applied to the cheap plated goods
and imitation jewellery once manufactured there and hence
came to mean 'cheap, tatty, showy'. An inhabitant of
Birmingham is known as a Brummie.

❯❯ Bubbles[1]

Although he was to become Admiral of the Fleet, William
James (1881–1973) is probably more famous for a portrait of
him as a four-year-old boy by his grandfather John Everett
Millais. The picture of a curly-headed boy blowing bubbles
became widely known when it was used in an advertisement
by Pears' soap. It was popularly known as 'Bubbles' and in
later life the name was applied to William James himself.

❯❯ Bubbles[2]

In 1955 the US operatic soprano Beverly Sills (b.1929) made
her debut with the New York City Opera. She retired to
become its general director in 1979, having been America's

leading opera star for over two decades. At the age of three she made her first public performance on the radio under the name of **Bubbles**, a nickname she gained at birth from a large bubble of saliva in her mouth. She has been known by the name all her life.

>> The Buckeye State

The US state of Ohio has an abundance of buckeye trees, an American tree related to the horse chestnut, with showy red or white flowers. Its fruit is supposed to resemble a deer's eye, hence the nickname **Buckeye State**. A Buckeye is a native of Ohio.

>> Buck House

Buck House is an informal name, dating from the early 1920s, for Buckingham Palace, the London residence of the British sovereign since 1837. Built in 1703 for the Duke of Buckingham, it was originally called Buckingham House.

>> Buddy

The US film and stage actor Marlon Brando (1924–2004) was a leading exponent of method acting. His early films included *A Streetcar Named Desire* (1951) and *On the Waterfront* (1954), for which he won an Academy Award. His later career included memorable roles in *The Godfather* (1972), *Last Tango in Paris* (1972), and *Apocalypse Now* (1979). **Buddy** was Brando's family nickname from childhood.

>> Bugsy Siegel

Benjamin Siegel (1906–47), the US racketeer and gangland killer, is often credited with founding the casino resort of Las Vegas in the Nevada Desert. His tendency to 'go bugs', that is, to fly into a violent rage, earned him the nickname **Bugsy** from his underworld acquaintances, though he would not tolerate its use in his presence.

▶▶ The Bullfrog of the Pontine Marshes

Benito Mussolini (1883–1945), Prime Minister of Italy
1922–43 and known as **Il Duce** ('the leader'), established a
totalitarian dictatorship and allied Italy with Germany,
entering the Second World War on Germany's side in 1940.
During the war Winston Churchill's scornful title for
Mussolini was the **Bullfrog of the Pontine Marshes**. This
refers to an area of reclaimed marshland in western Italy, on
the Tyrrhenian coast south of Rome.

▶▶ The Bullion State

Old Bullion was the nickname of Missouri senator Thomas
Hart Benton (1782–1858) because he advocated using
gold and silver in preference to paper currency. The
nickname the **Bullion State** subsequently transferred to the
state itself.

▶▶ Bull Moose

During the 1900 vice-presidential campaign, Theodore
Roosevelt (1858–1919) declared 'I am as strong as a bull
moose'. It was a phrase he would continue to use, and he
himself became known as **Bull Moose**. After serving two
terms as president, Roosevelt tried to make a comeback in
1912. Failing to win the Republican Party's presidential
nomination, he formed the Progressive Party to fight the
election. This new party became popularly known as the Bull
Moose Party.

▶▶ Bumble

The English cricketer David Lloyd (b.1947), who played for
Lancashire and England in the 1970s, is affectionately known
as **Bumble**. This is either because of his cheerful and
talkative personality or because his prominent nose was
thought to resemble those of the Bumblies, animated
characters from a BBC children's TV programme from 1954.

>> Bunny

Bunny is the traditional nickname in the British armed forces
for a man with the surname Austin or Austen. This comes
from the British tennis player 'Bunny' Austin, born Henry
Wilfred Austin (1906–2000), remembered as the first player
to wear shorts at Wimbledon. He picked up his nickname at
school, from a rabbit called Wilfred in a *Daily Sketch* cartoon
strip. Bunny is also a nickname often given to someone with
the surname Warren.

>> Buster

The nickname **Buster** is traditionally attached to the
surname Crabbe, after the US film actor Buster Crabbe
(1907–83), the **King of the Serials**, who in the 1930s was
cast in such comic-strip roles as Flash Gordon and Buck
Rogers. He was born Clarence Crabbe and picked up his
nickname as a boy. Another famous Buster is Buster Keaton
(1895–1966), the silent-film actor and director born Joseph
Francis Keaton. His nickname was given to him when, aged
six months, he tumbled down a flight of stairs in the
presence of the magician and escape artist Harry Houdini,
who said to his parents 'That's quite a buster your kid
took'.

>> The Butcher of Baghdad

Saddam Hussein (b.1937) was President of Iraq 1979–2003.
His Iraqi forces invaded and occupied Kuwait in August
1990, precipitating the Gulf War of 1991. Because of his
harsh treatment of Kurdish rebels in Iraq (involving the
use of chemical weapons against civilian populations) and
the atrocities reported to have been committed by the
army of occupation in Kuwait, Saddam was demonized as
the **Butcher of Baghdad** in the western popular press. He
was deposed as president following the 2003 war in
Iraq.

›› The Butcher of Broadway

From 1914 to 1922 Alexander Woollcott (1887–1943) was the drama critic of the *New York Times*. Famous for the savagery of some of his reviews, he was branded the **Butcher of Broadway**. Frank Rich (b.1949), chief theatre critic for the same newspaper from 1980 to 1993, earned the same nickname.

›› The Butcher of Lyons

The **Butcher of Lyons** was Klaus Barbie (1913–91), the head of the Gestapo in Lyons between 1942 and 1944, who is held to have been responsible for the deaths of 4,000 people and the deportation of over 7,000 others. Barbie was extradited from Bolivia to France in 1983 and in 1987 was tried in Lyons for 'crimes against humanity'. He was sentenced to life imprisonment.

➤➤ The Cabbage Garden

In Australia, the nickname the **Cabbage Garden** for the
state of Victoria dates from the 1920s and probably alludes to
its relatively small size or the crops grown there. It has also
been suggested that there may be a reference to the mallee, a
low-growing scrubby eucalyptus, that grows profusely in
the state. A later variant of the nickname is the **Cabbage
Patch**.

➤➤ The Canaries

Soon after the club's founding in 1902, Norwich City football
club acquired the nickname the **Canaries** from Norwich's
trade in breeding and exporting pet birds. They duly named
their ground The Nest and changed their strip to canary-
yellow shirts and green shorts.

➤➤ Cannibal

Eddy Merckx (b.1945), the Belgian racing cyclist, won the
Tour de France five times (1969–72 and 1974), also gaining
five victories in the Tour of Italy between 1968 and 1974. His
nickname the **Cannibal** came about because his strength and
endurance were such that he was thought to 'devour' his
opponents.

➤➤ The Cannonball Kid

The US tennis player Roscoe Tanner (b.1951) won the Australian Open in 1977 and was a Wimbledon finalist in 1979. Tanner was renowned for his powerful serve, earning himself the nickname the **Cannonball Kid**. Other hard-hitting players have had similar nicknames, such as Rod Laver (The **Rocket**), Pete Sampras (**Pistol Pete**) and Mark Philippoussis (The **Scud**).

➤➤ Captain Bob

Robert Maxwell. See ····➤ The **BOUNCING** Czech.

➤➤ Captain Marvel

In his playing days for Manchester United and England, the footballer Bryan Robson (b.1957) was known as **Captain Marvel**, after the US comic-book superhero. An inspirational captain of club and country, he won 90 international caps, 65 as England captain.

➤➤ Cat

The English cricketer Phil Tufnell (b.1966), a left-arm spin bowler for Middlesex and England, was nicknamed **Cat** by his Middlesex teammates because of his habit of taking naps during the day. The nickname dates from August 1988 when he neglected his duties as twelfth man by sleeping through the whole of the morning's session of play. In 2003 Tufnell was crowned 'King of the Jungle' when he won *I'm a Celebrity—Get Me Out of Here!*, a reality TV programme filmed in the Australian jungle.

➤➤ The Cat

Goalkeeper Peter Bonetti (b.1941), who played for Chelsea and England, was popularly known as the **Cat** because of his shot-saving agility.

❱❱ Cat's Eyes

The British fighter pilot John Cunningham (1917–2002)
became a group captain in 1944, making his name in
night-time defence against German bombers. His ability to
locate enemy planes in the dark was attributed to his
consumption of carrots, earning him his wartime nickname
Cat's Eyes, though Cunningham himself later put his
success down to the top secret radar on his Mosquito
aeroplane.

❱❱ The Centennial State

The US state of Colorado was admitted into the Union in
1876, a hundred years after the founding of the United
States, hence its nickname the **Centennial State**.

❱❱ The Chairboys

Wycombe Wanderers football club are called the **Chairboys**
because of High Wycombe's tradition of furniture-making.
The club was formed by a group of young furniture trade
workers in 1884.

❱❱ The Chairman of the Board

Between 1959 and 1963, Frank Sinatra (1915–98), the US
singer and film actor, was the acknowledged leader of the
'Rat Pack', a group of Las Vegas-based show-business friends
that also included Dean Martin, Sammy Davis Jr, Peter
Lawford, and Joey Bishop. Sinatra's status within the group
was reflected in his nicknames the **Chairman of the Board**,
the **Gov'nor**, and the **Pope**. The first of these was partly a
reference to his being the head of Reprise Records, a record
label he founded in 1961.

❱❱ Chalky

Chalky is one of the traditional nicknames in the British
armed forces of a man surnamed White, dating from the late

19th century. Another common nickname for someone called White used to be **Blanco**.

›› Chariots

Martin Offiah (b.1966), the British rugby league and rugby union player, was popularly known by the witty nickname **Chariots**. Offiah was noted for his speed as a winger and Chariots Offiah is a clever pun on the title of the 1981 film *Chariots of Fire*, which tells the story of the two British runners Eric Liddell and Harold Abrahams who won gold medals in the 1924 Olympics.

›› Charlie Hustle

The US baseball player Pete Rose (b.1941) was known as **Charlie Hustle** because of his habit of sprinting to first base even when he did not need to. Rose played for 24 years in the major leagues (1963–86), mainly with the Cincinnati Reds and the Philadelphia Phillies. He played in more games (3,562) and got more hits (4,256) than any player in baseball history.

›› The Cheeky Chappie

Max Miller (1895–1963), the British music-hall comedian, was billed as the **Cheeky Chappie**. Garishly dressed on stage in a multicoloured plus-four suit and white trilby, he was the master of the vulgar double entendre. His theme song 'Mary from the Dairy' began: 'I'm known as the Cheeky Chappie,/ The things I say are snappy./ That's why the pretty girls all fall for me.'

›› Cheggers

Keith Chegwin (b.1957), popularly known as **Cheggers**, appeared in various British children's TV programmes in the late 1970s, including a music show called *Cheggers Plays Pop*.

>> Chelski

Following the takeover of Chelsea football club by the
Russian billionaire tycoon Roman Abramovich in 2003, the
British media took to calling the club **Chelski**.

>> Chemical Ali

The Iraqi general Ali Hassan al-Majid (b.1938) earned his
notorious nickname **Chemical Ali** for ordering the use of
chemical weapons on Kurds in northern Iraq in 1988. He is
held responsible for the deaths of over 100,000 Kurds,
including 5,000 who died in a single day when Iraqi
forces used poison gas on the town of Halabja. The nickname
····▶ COMICAL Ali was based on this one.

>> Cheryl

Cheryl was the nickname used in the satirical magazine
Private Eye for Diana, Princess of Wales (1961–97).

>> The Chesterbelloc

The **Chesterbelloc** was a composite nickname, coined by
George Bernard Shaw, for G. K. Chesterton (1874–1936) and
Hilaire Belloc (1870–1953). The two writers collaborated on
a number of literary works and shared social and political
beliefs, in particular an opposition to the socialism of Shaw
and H. G. Wells. In 1908 Shaw published a lampoon
imagining Chesterton and Belloc as forming a single creature,
'a very amusing pantomime elephant', that he called 'the
Chesterbelloc'.

>> Chiantishire

Its popularity with English middle-class holiday-makers and
holiday-home buyers has earned the Italian region of Tuscany
the nickname **Chiantishire**, Chianti being a dry red Italian
wine produced in Tuscany. The term may have been coined
by the writer and barrister John Mortimer (b.1923).

›› The Chief[1]

The Irish statesman Eamon de Valera (1882–1975) was a giant of Irish politics for over half a century. He was involved in the Easter Rising, the leader of Sinn Fein 1917–26 and the founder of the Fianna Fáil Party in 1926. As President of the Irish Free State from 1932, de Valera was largely responsible for the new constitution of 1937 which created the state of Eire. He served as Taoiseach (Prime Minister) three times in the period 1937 to 1959 and then as President of the Republic of Ireland from 1959 to 1973. He was known in Ireland as the **Chief** and also as **Dev**.

›› The Chief[2]

Herbert C. Hoover (1874–1964) was the 31st President of the US 1929–33, his administration dominated by the Great Depression of the early 1930s. Earlier in his career he had organized food production and distribution in the US and Europe during and after the First World War. His success in this relief work earned him the title the **Chief**. He served as Secretary of Commerce under Presidents Harding and Coolidge (1921–28).

›› Chilly

The cricketer Chris Old (b.1948), a seam bowler for Yorkshire and England, was known as **Chilly** on the cricket field, from his name C. Old (i.e. *Cold*).

›› The Chingford Strangler

The British politician Norman Tebbit (b.1931) was formerly the Conservative MP for Chingford, Essex. Tebbit's abrasive style, outspoken views on race and immigration and his combative attacks on his political opponents earned him the nicknames the **Chingford Strangler** and the **Chingford Skinhead**. He was chairman of the Conservative Party 1985–87.

▶▶ The Chinook State

The **Chinook State** is the US state of Washington. The
Chinook are an American Indian people who originally lived
in the region around the mouth of the Columbia River. The
river flows through Washington state.

▶▶ The Choirboy

The British jockey Walter Swinburn (b.1961) was called the
Choirboy because of his cherubic appearance. He won his
first Derby in 1981, winning the race again in 1986 and
1995. In all, he rode eight Classic winners.

▶▶ Chopper

Ron Harris (b.1944) was one of the 'hard men' of English
football in the 1960s and 1970s. The Chelsea player was
known for his lunging tackles which were intended to 'chop
down' opponents, hence his nickname **Chopper**.

▶▶ Chu

The US jazz saxophonist Leon Berry (1910–41) came by the
nickname **Chu** in 1930 when his goatee beard caused fellow
musician Billy Stewart to remark that he looked oriental,
resembling the character Chu Chin Chow from the 1916
musical of that title based on the Ali Baba story.

▶▶ La Cicciolina

Ilona Staller (b.1955) is the Hungarian-born Italian porn
actress who was elected to the Italian parliament in 1987.
Her adopted name **La Cicciolina** means 'the little fleshy one'.

▶▶ The Cinderella Man

In the early 1930s James Braddock's (1906–74) boxing
career had taken such a downturn that he was surviving on
public welfare. Then in 1935 he made the most of his

opportunity to contest the world heavyweight title by, as a
15-1 outsider, unexpectedly defeating the champion Max
Baer. This rags-to-riches story caused Braddock to be dubbed
boxing's **Cinderella Man**.

❯❯ The City of Bon-accord

One of Aberdeen's nicknames is the **City of Bon-accord**. This
comes from *bon-accord*, which in Scottish usage (from
French) means 'good will, fellowship'.

❯❯ The City of Brotherly Love

In 1776 the Declaration of Independence was signed in
Philadelphia, Pennsylvania, and in 1787 the Constitution of
the United States was adopted in the same city. Philadelphia
literally means 'brotherly love', and the **City of Brotherly Love**
is an informal name for the city.

❯❯ The City of Dreaming Spires

Oxford is sometimes known as the **City of Dreaming Spires**, a
phrase that immediately conjures up the various steeples,
towers, and domes of the Oxford skyline. It is taken from the
poem 'Thyrsis' (1866) by Matthew Arnold: 'And that sweet
City with her dreaming Spires'. Some people prefer to call
Oxford the **City of Perspiring Dreams**.

❯❯ The City of Firsts

The **City of Firsts** is the US city of Kokomo, Indiana. Among
the innovations the city proudly claims are the first
mechanical corn-picker, the first push-button car radio, the
first commercially built car, and the first canned tomato juice.

❯❯ The City of Lilies

Lilies form part of the coat-of-arms of the Italian city of
Florence, hence its nickname the **City of Lilies**.

❯❯ The City of Magnificent Distances

The US city of Washington DC boasts numerous parks, wide avenues, and impressive vistas, and is sometimes known as the **City of Magnificent Distances**. The nickname was coined in 1816 by the Portuguese Minister to the United States, José Correa da Serra.

❯❯ The City of Saints

Because many of its streets are named after saints Montreal is known as the **City of Saints**. The same phrase has been applied to Salt Lake City, Utah, the world headquarters of the Church of Latter-Day Saints.

❯❯ The City of the Seven Hills

The **City of the Seven Hills** (*Urbs Septacollis*) is Rome. This is because the ancient city of Rome was built on seven hills, namely Aventine, Caelian, Capitoline, Esquilane, Quirinal, Viminal, and Palatine.

❯❯ Clockwork Ocwirk

One of the great rhyming nicknames belongs to the Austrian footballer Ernst Ocwirk (b.1926). A creative midfield player, Ocwirk played for FK Austria and the Italian club Sampdoria. He first played for Austria in 1947 and went on to win 62 caps. After his impressive performance at Wembley when Austria drew 2–2 against England in 1951, the British press were quick to dub him **Clockwork Ocwirk**.

❯❯ The Clones Cyclone

The boxer Barry McGuigan (b.1961) was brought up in Clones, County Monaghan, on the border between the Republic of Ireland and Northern Ireland. Under the ring name the **Clones Cyclone**, he became WBA featherweight champion in 1985.

❯❯ The Clothes Horse

Joan Crawford (1908–77) was one of Hollywood's leading
film stars for over forty years. She came to be associated with
sultry roles in psychological melodramas and starred in such
films as *Rain* (1932), *The Women* (1939), and *Mildred Pierce*
(1945), for which she won an Academy Award. Crawford was
dubbed the **Clothes Horse** because of her lavish wardrobe,
even during the Depression.

❯❯ The Clown Prince of Basketball

In 1954 Meadowlark Lemon (b.1933) joined the Harlem
Globetrotters, a professional basketball team who tour the
world giving exhibition matches combining ball skills with
comedy routines. He became the star of the team and came
to be known as the **Clown Prince of Basketball**.

❯❯ The Coathanger

Australians sometimes call Sydney Harbour Bridge (opened
in 1932) the **Coat Hanger** because of its distinctive shape. Its
main arch is 503m (1,652 ft) long.

❯❯ The Cobblers

Northampton Town football club are known as the
Cobblers on account of the town's once-dominant shoe- and
boot-making industry. A fanzine dedicated to the football
club is perhaps inevitably titled *What a Load of Cobblers*.

❯❯ The Cockpit of Europe

Belgium has been described as the **Cockpit of Europe** because
so many European conflicts have been fought there. Battles
fought on Belgian soil have included Ramilles (1706),
Waterloo (1815), Mons and Ypres in the First World War, and
the German invasion of 1940. The term *cockpit*, historically
an enclosure used for holding cockfights, can be applied to
any arena of conflict.

›› The Comeback Kid

Bill Clinton (b.1946) first called himself the **Comeback Kid** in
1992, following the Democratic primary in New Hampshire.
Charges of womanizing and draft-dodging badly damaged his
campaign, and he came a poor second to another candidate
Paul Tsongas. Since 1952 every US president had won his
party's New Hampshire primary so this defeat appeared to
cast serious doubt on Clinton's presidential ambitions. The
phrase, encapsulating Clinton's determination to recover
from this apparent setback, was actually coined by his
campaign strategist Paul Begala. Clinton went on to win the
Democratic presidential nomination and was elected
president in November 1992. The nickname proved
appropriate during Clinton's presidency, as he sought to
bounce back from further reverses, in particular allegations
of financial impropriety during his period in office in
Arkansas, sex scandals, and ultimately impeachment
proceedings.

›› Comical Ali

Ali Mohammed Saeed al-Sahaf (b.1940) was the Iraqi
minister of information during the war in Iraq in 2003. He
was dubbed **Comical Ali** (a nickname based on ····► CHEMICAL
Ali) when his defiantly optimistic denials of US and British
military advances made him a cult figure in the Western
media. Al-Sahaf refused to admit that US troops were in
Baghdad even when the rumbling of tanks and the sound of
gunfire could be heard just half a mile away.

›› Conan the Republican

Arnold Schwarzenegger. See ····► The GOVERNATOR.

›› The Constitution State

Connecticut's official nickname is the **Constitution State**.
This is because the Fundamental Orders drawn up in

Hartford in 1639 are believed to be the first formal constitution written on American soil. The draft US constitution was partly based on this and was itself ratified in Connecticut in 1788.

▶▶ The Cornhusker State

Nebraska is known as the **Cornhusker State**. The term Cornhusker, originally applied to the University of Nebraska's athletics and football teams, is used for any native or resident of Nebraska.

▶▶ The Cottagers

Fulham football club have played at Craven Cottage since 1896, hence their nickname the **Cottagers**. Since May 2002 the club have groundshared at Queens Park Rangers' Loftus Road stadium while Craven Cottage has been redeveloped.

▶▶ The Cotton State

Cotton-growing was at one time a dominant part of Alabama's economy, hence the state's nickname the **Cotton State**.

▶▶ Count

Among the jazz aristocracy, Edward Kennedy Ellington is the Duke and William James Basie (1904–84) is the Count. The big band Basie formed in 1935, the Count Basie Orchestra, was an influential band of the swing era, noted for its strong rhythm section. Bill Basie was probably given the nickname **Count** by a Kansas City radio announcer in the 1930s, though there is some evidence that he had given himself the title earlier, even having business cards printed with the words 'Beware the Count is Here'.

›› The Cowboy Philosopher

Will Rogers (1879–1935) began his career as a rodeo cowboy
and rope-twirler in vaudeville shows such as the Ziegfeld
Follies. He also appeared in films. He later became a
perceptive political commentator, known for his aphorisms
and homespun wisdom. Rogers' popular newspaper articles
and columns were eventually syndicated, reaching an
estimated audience of 40 million readers. He was widely
known as the **Cowboy Philosopher**.

›› The Coyote State

South Dakota's official nickname the **Coyote State** comes
from the name of the wolflike wild dog native to western
North America and also known as the prairie wolf. The
term Coyote is also used to denote an inhabitant of South
Dakota.

›› The Crab

The English footballer Ray Wilkins (b.1956) played for a
number of clubs including Chelsea, Manchester United, and
Milan, and won 84 England caps. Complaining that the
player was over-cautious, manager Ron Atkinson nicknamed
him the **Crab** for continually passing the ball sideways: 'the
only time he goes forward is to toss the coin'.

›› The Cracker State

The US state of Georgia has enjoyed the nickname the
Cracker State since the late 19th century. The reason for this
is not entirely certain. It may come from early settlers
cracking their whips over their mules or from the practice of
cracking corn to make cornmeal or even from the harsh
Georgian dialect, sometimes thought to resemble a cracking
sound.

›› The Cradle of Liberty

The city of Boston in Massachusetts was the centre of opposition to the British before and during the War of American Independence, hence its nickname the **Cradle of Liberty**.

›› The Crafty Cockney

Eric Bristow (b.1957) was the leading darts player of the early 1980s. He won the world championship in 1980, going on to win a further four world titles (1981, 1984, 1985, 1986). According to the London-born Bristow, he took his nickname from a shirt given to him by the owner of the *Crafty Cockney* bar in Beverley Hills.

›› Crawfie

Marion Crawford (1909–88), known in the press as **Crawfie**, was the governess to the Princesses Elizabeth and Margaret in the 1930s. The unauthorized publication of her reminiscences in 'The Little Princesses', an article that appeared in *Women's Own* magazine, caused her to fall out of royal favour.

›› Crazy Horse

The footballer Emlyn Hughes (b.1947) played for Liverpool and England, winning 62 international caps (23 as captain). His whole-hearted enthusiasm and stamina led his Liverpool teammates to call him **Crazy Horse**. The historical Crazy Horse was a Sioux chief Ta-Sunko-Witko (c.1849–77), leader of the Indian force that defeated General Custer at Little Bighorn in 1876.

›› Crescent City

New Orleans, Louisiana, is nicknamed **Crescent City** because of the city's location on the east bank of a bend in the Mississippi River.

›› The Crocodile

The New Zealand physicist Ernest Rutherford (1871–1937) is regarded as the founder of nuclear physics. Working with him at the Cavendish laboratories in Cambridge, the Russian physicist Peter Kapitza (1894–1984) used to call Rutherford the **Crocodile**. Kapitza's explanation was that it was a name often given to great men in Russian folklore. The real reason was probably more mischievous: just as the crocodile in *Peter Pan* could be heard approaching by the ticking of Captain Hook's watch that it had swallowed, so Rutherford's arrival was usually preceded by the sound of his booming voice. In Rutherford's honour, Kapitza commissioned the sculptor Eric Gill to carve a crocodile on the outer wall of one of the Cavendish laboratories.

›› Cuddly Ken

Kenny Everett (1944–95), the British disc jockey and comedian, made his name as an anarchic DJ, initially on pirate radio, before transferring his zany brand of humour to television in the late 70s and early 80s. Everett used to refer to himself as **Cuddly Ken**.

›› CuJo

The Canadian ice hockey player Curtis Joseph (b.1967) has played goaltender for the St Louis Blues, the Edmonton Oilers, the Toronto Maple Leafs, and the Detroit Red Wings. His St Louis Blues teammates gave Joseph the nickname **CuJo** (or **Cujo**), from the first two letters of his first and last names and also a reference to the name of the rabid St Bernard dog in the Stephen King novel *Cujo* (1981). Joseph's helmet has a fanged dog design painted on it. The South American Indian word *cujo* means 'unstoppable force'.

›› Curly

Curly is sometimes used as a nickname for someone with

curly hair. More perversely, bald-headed men can be called Curly too. Curly Howard (1903–52) was the bald member of the Three Stooges, a US comedy act. His real name was Jerome.

›› The Currant Bun

The Sun newspaper is informally known in southern England as the **Currant Bun**. This is Cockney rhyming slang for 'sun'.

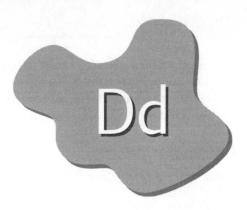

⟩⟩ Dame Harold

Harold Evans (b.1928) edited *The Sunday Times* (1967–81) and *The Times* (1981–82), and later went on to run the Random House publishing group in the US. While editor of *The Sunday Times*, he was dubbed **Dame Harold Evans** by Lord Arran because he was thought to look like the great theatrical Dame, Edith Evans. The nickname was gleefully taken up by the satirical magazine *Private Eye*.

⟩⟩ The Dancing Destroyer

The Nigerian-born British boxer Herbie Hide (b.1971) became WBO heavyweight champion 1994–95. His style in the ring was characterized by his fast hands and nimble footwork, which was why he was promoted as the **Dancing Destroyer**.

⟩⟩ The Dapper Don

Mafia boss John Gotti (1940–2002) was known by the New York tabloids as the **Dapper Don** because of his expensively tailored Italian suits. In 1992 he was finally convicted of murder, racketeering, and conspiracy and died in prison of throat cancer having served ten years of a life sentence.

⟩⟩ The Dark and Bloody Ground

This name for Kentucky was made popular by the US poet Theodore O'Hara (1820–67): 'Sons of the dark and bloody ground' ('The Bivouac of the Dead', 1847). The phrase is said to come from a warning given by a Cherokee chief in the late 18th century, that the land was already 'a bloody ground' because of fierce battles fought between American Indian tribes and that it would be dark for prospective settlers.

Darts Players

No self-respecting professional darts player is without a colourful nickname. Here is a selection of some current players' monikers:

the Artist — Kevin Painter (from his surname)

Barney — Raymond Van Barneveld (from his surname. Also **Barney Rubble**, as in *The Flintstones* cartoon)

the Bronze Adonis — Steve Beaton (persona as 'the most handsome man in darts'. According to commentator Sid Waddell: 'He's not Adonis, he's THE Donis.')

the Count — Ted Hankey (Dracula-like appearance, makes his entrance in a cape)

Hawaii 501 — Wayne Mardle (wears bright shirts)

John Boy — John Walton (as in the character from the US TV series *The Waltons*)

the King — Mervyn King (from his surname. Also **Merv the Swerve**)

the Matchstick — Co Stompe (slim, bald head. Also the **Pencil**)

the Power — Phil Taylor (has dominated the sport in recent years)

the Viking — Andy Fordham (hairy beard, long hair, large frame)

» The Darling of the Halls

The music-hall comedian George Robey (1869–1954) became known as the **Darling of the Halls** following a famous courtroom exchange. In response to Mr Justice Darling's enquiry 'And who is George Robey?', the lawyer (later statesman) F. E. Smith (1872–1930) replied: 'Mr George Robey is the Darling of the music halls, m'lud'.

» Dazzler

Darren Gough (b.1970), the Yorkshire and England cricketer, is nicknamed **Dazzler**. It's a name that suits his ebullient personality, his lively fast bowling, and his cavalier batting. He had earlier been known as **Guzzler** because of his large appetite.

» Deadly[1]

Doug Ellis (b.1924) became chairman of Aston Villa football club in December 1968. He was nicknamed **Deadly** because it was said that he sacked a succession of managers, though, in fact, a number of managers who left the club during this tenure were not sacked but chose to resign.

» Deadly[2]

The English cricketer Derek Underwood (b.1945) was a left-arm spin bowler for Kent and England. The accuracy and relentless consistency of Underwood's bowling earned him the nickname **Deadly**.

» Der Alte

At the age of 73, Konrad Adenauer (1876–1967) became the first Chancellor of the Federal Republic of Germany in 1949. He went on to preside over the political and economic reconstruction of his country after the Second World War. Adenauer was known in Germany as **Der Alte** or 'the Old Man'. In 1963, he finally resigned as Chancellor at the age of 87.

▶▶ Der Bingle

The US singer and film actor Bing Crosby (1904–77) was
known by German soldiers in the Second World War as **Der
Bingle**. Born Harry Lillis Crosby, the singer got the name Bing
from his big ears. As a child he used to read a comic book
called *The Bingville Bugle* which featured a character called
Bingo, a boy with large, floppy ears.

▶▶ The Desert Fox

The German field marshal Erwin Rommel (1891–1944)
commanded the Afrika Korps in North Africa in the Second
World War. He became known as the **Desert Fox** for
outwitting Allied forces with a series of surprise manoeuvres.
He succeeded in capturing Tobruk (1942), but was defeated
by Montgomery at El Alamein later that year. Rommel was
forced to commit suicide after being implicated in the
officers' plot against Hitler in 1944.

▶▶ Diamond City

The city of Amsterdam is a major centre of the diamond-
cutting industry, hence its nickname **Diamond City**.

▶▶ Diamond Jim

James Buchanan Brady (1856–1917) started out as a bellboy
in a New York hotel, later rising from a job as railway worker
to amass a fortune selling railway equipment. He was known
as **Diamond Jim** because of his extravagant tastes and
fondness for wearing diamond jewellery, for example shirt-
studs, tie-pins, and cuff-links.

▶▶ The Diamond State

The US state of Delaware is known as the **Diamond State**.
Though small in size (only Rhode Island is smaller),
Delaware has great historical importance: it was the first of
the thirteen founding states of the Union.

›› Dickie

Dickie is a common nickname for any man with the surname Bird. The most famous recent example is the cricket umpire Harold Bird (b.1933), universally known as Dickie Bird.

›› Dinty

Dinty is a traditional nickname of people with the surname Moore. This comes from the character of the tavern keeper Dinty Moore in the early 20th-century US comic strip *Bringing Up Father*. In the 1930s Dinty Moore was adopted as the brandname of a line of tinned stew and other canned foods.

›› Dippermouth

Jazz fans know Louis Armstrong as **Satchmo** or **Satch**, which came from **Satchelmouth**, a name for a person with a large mouth. An earlier nickname for the musician was **Dippermouth**. Here Armstrong's mouth was being compared to a dipper, that is a ladle or long-handled pan. In 1923 King Oliver's band (with whom Armstrong then played) recorded 'Dippermouth Blues', which may have been named after him.

›› The Dirty Digger

Rupert Murdoch (b.1931), the Australian-born newspaper and media tycoon, is sometimes referred to in the UK as the **Dirty Digger**. In Australia and New Zealand, *digger* is an informal term for a man, especially a private soldier. The term derived (in the early 20th century) from digger 'miner', reinforced by association with the digging of trenches on the battlefields.

›› The Divine Callas

The opera singer Maria Callas (1923–77), born in New York of Greek parents, became known as the **Divine Callas**. Often acknowledged as the greatest singing actress of the 20th century, Callas is celebrated for the intensity of her acting and the power and range of her voice. Her bel canto style of singing especially suited her to early Italian opera and she excelled in such roles as Bellini's Norma, Cherubini's Medea, and Puccini's Tosca.

❯❯ The Divine Miss M

The **Divine Miss M** was the persona that the singer, comedienne, and actress Bette Midler (b.1945) created for her outrageous stage act, developed early on in her career when she performed at gay venues in New York City. She performed the role of a brassy and bawdy cabaret star modelled on the likes of Mae West and Sophie Tucker. Midler's first album was entitled *The Divine Miss M* (1972). She also liked to refer to herself as the **Last of the Tacky Ladies**.

❯❯ The Divine One

The US jazz singer and pianist Sarah Vaughan (1924–90) was acclaimed for her vocal range and improvisational skills. She became an international star recording both jazz numbers and romantic ballads. Sometimes described as jazz's diva, Vaughan was called **Sassy** by those who knew her and the **Divine One** by her many admirers.

❯❯ The Divine Ponytail

The Italian footballer Roberto Baggio (b.1967) was nicknamed the **Divine Ponytail** because of the hairstyle he wore for much of his career. Baggio played for Italy in three World Cup tournaments and was named both World and European Player of the Year in 1993. The clubs he has played for include Fiorentina, Juventus, AC Milan, Bologna, and Inter Milan.

❯❯ The Divine Sarah

It was Oscar Wilde who first called the celebrated French actress Sarah Bernhardt (1844–1923) the **Divine Sarah**. Internationally acclaimed as the greatest tragic actress of her day, she was noted for her great beauty, the clarity of her speaking voice, and her charismatic personality. Although she had one of her legs amputated in 1915, she continued to act until her death.

>> Dixie

The footballer Dixie Dean (1907–80) made his debut for Everton in 1925 and is remembered for scoring 60 league goals for the club in the 1927–28 season, a tally for a season that has never been beaten. He was born William Ralph Dean but apparently came by the nickname **Dixie** because of his swarthy complexion, thought to resemble that of inhabitants of the southern USA, known as Dixieland. Dean hated his nickname but it has subsequently been applied to many other men sharing his surname.

>> Dizzy

The US jazz trumpeter and band-leader Dizzy Gillespie (1917–93) was a leading exponent of the bebop style. Born John Birks Gillespie, he picked up his nickname **Dizzy** when playing with the Frankie Fairfax band in Philadelphia in 1935, because he used to clown around on stage.

>> The Doc

The Scottish football manager Tommy Docherty (b.1928) managed a succession of clubs, including Chelsea, Queen's Park Rangers, Aston Villa, and Manchester United, once joking that he had 'had more clubs than Jack Nicklaus'. Known for his forthright views on the game, Docherty's managerial career was often marked by controversy. His nickname the **Doc** is an abbreviation of his surname.

>> The Dockers' KC

As secretary of the dock workers' union, Ernest Bevin (1881–1951) successfully argued the dockers' case for higher

wages and better conditions before the Commission of
Inquiry of 1920. This won him the nickname the **Dockers' KC**
(that is, King's Counsel). Bevin was one of the founders of
the Transport and General Workers' Union, serving as its first
General Secretary (1921–40), and was a leading organizer of
the General Strike (1926). He was later to serve as Foreign
Secretary (1945–51).

›› Dolly

Basil d'Oliveira (b.1931), known as **Dolly**, played for England
in 44 Test matches. At the start of the 1968 MCC tour of
South Africa, d'Oliveira was the central figure in an
international incident when the South African-born player
was refused entry to the country because he was a 'Cape
Coloured'. As a result the tour was cancelled.

›› The Don

The Australian cricketer Donald Bradman (1908–2001) was
an outstanding batsman who dominated the sport in his day.
He played for his country from 1928 until his retirement in
1948, captaining Australia from 1936 to 1948. A prolific run-
maker, Bradman scored 117 first-class centuries, 29 of them
in Test matches. His Test match batting average of 99.94 is
well above that of any other cricketer of any era. Although
generally known as the **Don** (from his first name), he was
also nicknamed the **Little Master** because of his relatively
diminutive stature.

›› The Donald

Donald Trump (b.1946), the US billionaire property
developer and businessman, is popularly known as the
Donald, which is what Ivana Trump, his Czech-born first
wife, used to call him.

▶▶ The Doog

During the 1960s and 1970s, the footballer Derek Dougan
(b.1938) made 244 league appearances for Wolverhampton
Wanderers, scoring 95 goals. The centre forward, who won
43 caps for Northern Ireland, was popularly known by the
Wolverhampton fans as the **Doog**.

▶▶ Doris Karloff

Doris Karloff is the name used by the British tabloids to refer
to the Conservative politician Ann Widdecombe (b.1947). In
the 1990s, as a Home Office minister with responsibility for
prisons, she acquired a reputation for uncompromising
toughness and combativeness. This, together with her
somewhat dour appearance, inspired her nickname, based on
the name of the horror-film actor Boris Karloff (1887–1969).
She has been known to answer the phone with the words
'Karloff here'.

▶▶ Dracula[1]

The Welsh snooker player Ray Reardon (b.1932) won the
world championship in 1970, 1973–76, and 1978. He was
known as **Dracula** because of his facial resemblance to movie
incarnations of Bram Stoker's fictional vampire and his
prominent eye-teeth.

▶▶ Dracula[2]

When Michael Howard (b.1941) declared himself a candidate
for the leadership of the Conservative Party in 2003, the
Daily Mirror ran the headline 'Dracula Stakes his Claim'.
Howard's nickname comes partly from his Transylvanian
ancestry and partly from his fellow MP Ann Widdecombe's
widely quoted remark in 1997 that he had 'something of the
night about him'. In his first speech as Conservative leader he
said that for Labour MPs 'words like choice and competition
are as welcome as a clove of garlic to Dracula'.

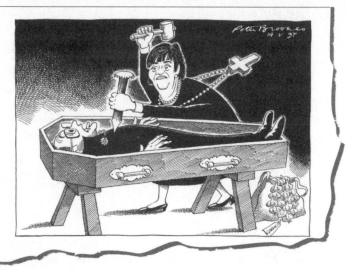

3. Michael Howard as Dracula, 1997

›› Dr Death[1]

David Owen (b.1938) served as Foreign Secretary 1977–79 in the Labour government. Growing increasingly dissatisfied with the Labour Party's policies, in 1981 he broke away to become a founding member of the Social Democratic Party (SDP). He led the SDP from 1983 to 1987, resigning to form a breakaway SDP when the main party decided to merge with the Liberals. Owen's nickname **Dr Death** referred to his earlier career as a neurologist, to his dark, brooding looks, and to his alleged political ruthlessness.

›› Dr Death[2]

Harold Shipman (1946–2004) was Britain's worst serial killer. A general practitioner from Hyde in Greater Manchester, he was sentenced to life imprisonment in 2000 for the murders of 15 patients, mainly elderly women, by lethal injections of the drug diamorphine. A subsequent inquiry concluded that he had been responsible for the deaths of at least 215 patients over a 23-year period. During Shipman's trial the British tabloids dubbed him **Dr Death**.

›› Dr J

Basketball player Julius Erving (b.1950) scored over 30,000 points in his professional career, winning the NBA championship with the Philadelphia 76ers in 1983. He had formerly been a star of the ABA, before it folded. While at Roosevelt High School, Erving called his teammate and friend Leon Saunders the **Professor**, who dubbed him the **Doctor** in return. This was later modified to **Dr J** when Erving attended the University of Massachusetts. The nickname seemed to suit Erving's surgical efficiency on a basketball court.

›› Dubya

George Walker Bush (b.1946) became president of the US in 2001. To distinguish him from his father, the former president George Bush, the son is widely known as George W. Bush, or simple as George W. The nickname **Dubya** represents

4. Dubya

the Texan pronunciation of the letter W. Another way to differentiate between the two presidents has been to refer to one as '41' (i.e. the 41st US president) and the other as '43'.

▶▶ Dugout Doug

The US general Douglas MacArthur (1880–1964) commanded the US defence of the Philippines against the Japanese 1941–42. The front line troops under heavy bombardment on the Bataan peninsula felt that MacArthur, conducting operations from his underground shelter on Corregidor Island, had abandoned them. Their scathing name for him, **Dugout Doug**, pursued him for the rest of the war.

▶▶ Duke[1]

The composer and bandleader Duke Ellington (1899–1974) was one of the leading figures in the history of jazz and has been described as the greatest composer that jazz has ever produced. He wrote over 900, often complex, compositions, including 'Mood Indigo' and 'Satin Doll'. The musician was born Edward Kennedy Ellington and was first called **Duke** by his school friends, apparently because he was always so elegantly dressed and had a somewhat aristocratic bearing.

▶▶ Duke[2]

John Wayne (1907–79) is chiefly associated with roles in such westerns as *Stagecoach* (1939), *Red River* (1948), and *True Grit* (1969). He came by the nickname **Duke** in childhood, when he was still known by his real name of Marion Morrison. Duke was the name of the family's pet dog, an Airedale terrier. When as a boy he walked the dog around the neighbourhood, people referred to the dog and his master as Little Duke and Big Duke respectively. The childhood name stuck and he began his film career in 1927 under the name Duke Morrison. Although he soon changed this to John

Wayne, he continued to be known as Duke, a nickname that
well suited the tough, plain-speaking roles he played.

›› Dusty

The nickname **Dusty** is traditionally attached to the surname
Miller, from the idea that a miller is always dusty from the
corn dust. A 1788 song by Robert Burns is called 'The Dusty
Miller': 'Dusty was the coat,/Dusty was the colour,/Dusty was
the kiss/That I gat frae the Miller.' People surnamed Rhodes
are also sometimes given the nickname Dusty.

›› Dutch[1]

Marlene Dietrich (1901–92), the German-born US film
actress and singer, won international fame in the 1930
German film *Der Blaue Engel* (*The Blue Angel*). Her
Hollywood films include *Morocco* (1930), *Shanghai Express*
(1932), and *Destry Rides Again* (1939). From the 1950s she
was an internationally successful cabaret star, noted for her
husky, sultry singing voice. Among her circle of friends in
Hollywood, she was affectionately known as **Dutch**, a
humorous corruption of *Deutsche* 'German'.

›› Dutch[2]

Ronald Reagan (1911–2004), President of the US 1981–89,
has been known as **Dutch** all his life. According to Reagan's
own account, this family nickname came from his father's
remark after his birth: 'For such a little bit of a fat Dutchman,
he makes a hell of a lot of noise.'

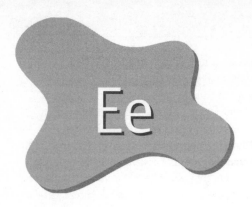

Ee

➤➤ Earl the Pearl

Earl Monroe (b.1944), known as **Earl the Pearl** (or simply the **Pearl**), played basketball for the Baltimore Bullets and the New York Knicks, with whom he won the NBA championship in 1973. He is remembered for his dazzling ball-handling and flamboyant style.

➤➤ Eddie the Eagle

Eddie Edwards (b.1963) shot to fame at the 1988 Winter Olympics in Calgary when his hopeless ski-jumping performance representing Britain made him a folk-hero. He came 56th in a field of 57 competitors, the 57th having been disqualified. At the closing ceremony, the IOC president Juan Antonio Samaranch singled out the ski-jumper's heroic failure for special mention: 'At this Olympic Games some competitors have won gold, some have broken records, and one has even flown like an Eagle.' Edwards' nickname inspired that of the similarly hopeless ····➤ **ERIC** the Eel.

➤➤ Edward the Caresser

Edward VII (1841–1910) was a notorious womanizer. So, rather than Edward the Confessor, he was sometimes known as **Edward the Caresser**.

➤➤ Edward the Peacemaker

Edward VII (1841–1910) was nicknamed **Edward the**

Peacemaker in recognition of his efforts in diplomacy. Related to many of the crowned heads of Europe, Edward used his visits abroad to help prevent the outbreak of a European war. The *Entente Cordiale* between Britain and France was established in his reign. His affair with Lillie Langtry earned him the punning alternative nickname **Edward the Piecemaker**.

➤➤ Eisenhower Platz

During the Second World War, Grosvenor Square in the West End of London, where the US embassy is situated, was informally known as **Eisenhower Platz**. Many of its buildings were occupied by the headquarters of the US military forces in Europe, under the command of General Dwight D. Eisenhower. Another nickname for the square was ····➤ **LITTLE** America.

➤➤ El Beatle

With his good looks, charisma, and high-living lifestyle, George Best (b.1946) was the first British footballing superstar, a sporting equivalent of the Beatles rock group. An exceptionally skilful striker and winger, Best made his debut for Manchester United in 1963 at the age of 17 and made 349 league appearances for them over the next ten years. In 1966 the British press dubbed him **El Beatle** when he was photographed wearing an enormous sombrero on the team's triumphant return from Portugal having beaten the Lisbon club Benfica 5–1.

➤➤ El Tel

Although Terry Venables (b.1943) is by no means the only British football manager to have worked in Spain, his affectionate and tabloid-friendly nickname is a reference to his time as coach of Barcelona FC (1984–87), during which period the club won the Spanish league title. When he later returned to English football to manage Tottenham Hotspur and subsequently to coach the England national side (1994–96), he continued to be popularly known as **El Tel**.

❯❯ Elvis the Pelvis

Elvis Presley (1935–77), the US pop and rock-and-roll singer, shot to fame in 1956 with such records as 'Heartbreak Hotel', 'Blue Suede Shoes' and 'Hound Dog'. His performances on stage were noted for their vigorous sexuality and for the suggestive hip gyrations which inspired his nickname. When he first appeared on national television he was shown only from the waist up.

❯❯ The Emerald Isle

The **Emerald Isle** is Ireland. The name, referring to the lush green of Ireland's countryside, is first recorded in the nationalist poem *Erin* by William Drennan (1754–1820): 'Nor one feeling of vengeance presume to defile/The cause, or the men, of the Emerald Isle' (1795).

❯❯ Empire City

New York City takes its nickname **Empire City** from that of New York State, the **Empire State**.

❯❯ The Empire State

In 1784 George Washington referred to the state of New York as 'the seat of Empire', the origin of its nickname (dating from *c.*1820) the **Empire State**.

❯❯ The Empress of Emotion

Elissa Landi (1904–48) was an Austrian-Italian film actress who made films in several countries before becoming a Hollywood leading lady in the 1930s, starring in such films as *The Sign of the Cross* (1932) and *The Count of Monte Cristo* (1934).

❯❯ The Empress of the Blues

Bessie Smith (1894–1937) established herself as the pre-eminent female singer of the blues in the 1920s and made over 150 recordings. She is remembered for the strength and intensity of her voice and the vitality of her performances. A hugely influential singer, she is the unchallenged **Empress of the Blues**.

❯❯ The Equality State

In 1869 Wyoming became the first state in the US to grant votes to women, hence its nickname the **Equality State**. An earlier variation was the **Suffrage State**.

❯❯ Eric the Eel

At the 2000 Sydney Olympic Games, the Equatorial Guinean swimmer Eric Moussambani (b.1980) swam a heat of the 100m freestyle in a time of 1 minute 52.72 seconds, one of the slowest times in Olympic history. He became an overnight celebrity, his nickname deliberately modelled on that of ····▶ **EDDIE** the Eagle.

❯❯ The Eternal City

The Italian city of Rome has been known as the **Eternal City** since classical times, a translation of Latin *urbs aeterna*, a phrase used by Ovid and Tibullus, and frequently found in the official documents of the Empire.

❯❯ Evans of the Broke

The British admiral and explorer Edward Evans, 1st Baron Mountevans (1881–1957) became known as **Evans of the Broke** after an incident in the First World War when, as commander of HMS *Broke* (pronounced 'brook'), he sank six German destroyers.

›› The Evergreen State

The mountains of the US state of Washington are covered by forests of spruce and Douglas fir, reflected not only in the state's nickname but also in its green flag. The **Evergreen State** was adopted as Washington's official nickname in 1893.

›› Evita

After her husband Juan Perón became president of Argentina in 1946, Eva Perón (1919–52) effectively became Minister of Health and of Labour. In this capacity she organized female workers, secured the vote for women, and earmarked substantial government funds for social welfare. Idolized by the Argentine public for her charitable work, she was popularly known as **Evita**. She died of cancer at the age of 33. The stage musical *Evita*, based on her life, is by Andrew Lloyd Webber and Tim Rice.

›› Famous Seamus

The Irish poet Seamus Heaney (b.1939) was awarded the Nobel Prize for Literature in 1995. His subsequent celebrity has won him the rhyming nickname **Famous Seamus** in Irish literary circles. Among his collections are *North* (1975), *The Haw Lantern* (1987), and *Spirit Level* (1996).

›› Fatha

The jazz pianist Earl Hines (1905–83) formed his own band in 1929, later playing with Louis Armstrong's All Stars (1948–51). While such members of the jazz nobility as Duke Ellington, Count Basie, and King Oliver owe their titles to nicknames, Earl Hines was born with that name. His own nickname of **Fatha** was originally given to him by the radio announcer/engineer Ted Pearson.

›› The Father of the Atomic Bomb

The US physicist Robert Oppenheimer (1904–67) has been called the **Father of the Atomic Bomb**. As director of the laboratory at Los Alamos, New Mexico, during the Second World War, he supervised the development and construction of the first atomic bomb, known as the Manhattan Project. Oppenheimer later opposed the development of the hydrogen bomb.

Fat

Obesity has always attracted nicknames, often unkind ones. Among the handles a fat person has traditionally been saddled with are:

Billy Bunter, **Chubby**, **Fat Boy**, **Fats**, **Fatso**, **Fatty**, **Fatty Arbuckle** (or **Harbuckle**), **Jabba the Hutt** (from the *Star Wars* character), **Jumbo**, **Lardass**, **Piggy**, **Podge**, **Porky**, and **Tubby**. As with other nicknames relating to physical traits, many of these terms can also be used simply as insults or taunts. Royalty has by no means been exempt. Two French kings, Charles III and Louis VI were both known as **The Fat**. And George, the Prince Regent (later George IV), was nicknamed the **Prince of Whales**. His successor as Prince of Wales, the future Edward VII, was called **Tum-Tum**. Nicknames included in this book that draw attention to the person's bulk include **Jessyenormous**, (Jessye Norman);
Two Dinners (Lord Goodman);
Two-Ton Tessie (Tessie O'Shea); and the
Walrus of Love (Barry White).
See also ····▶ FATS and ····▶ FATTY.

▶▶ The Father of the Blues

W. C. Handy (1873–1958), the US blues musician, composer, and bandleader, became known as the **Father of the Blues**, which was also to be the title of his 1941 autobiography.

Although by no means the first musician to play the blues, he was one of the first to write this music down in such compositions as 'Memphis Blues' (1912), one of the first blues ever published, and 'St Louis Blues' (1914). Many of these compositions were inspired by the rural blues songs Handy had heard and were not therefore entirely original, a fact he readily acknowledged. Handy's reputation as the originator of the blues (and indeed jazz) has been scornfully disputed by many, notably Jelly Roll Morton.

▶▶ The Father of the Hole

Henry Moore (1898–1986) is known for his massive semi-abstract sculptures, typically of reclining forms and family groups, which characteristically have holes or hollows within them. Because of these empty spaces in his work Moore has been dubbed the **Father of the Hole**.

▶▶ The Father of the Skyscraper

The title the **Father of the Skyscraper** is shared by two US architects, William Le Baron Jenney (1832–1907) and Cass Gilbert (1859–1934). Jenney designed the first steel-frame building, the 10-storey Home Insurance Building in Chicago (1883), usually regarded as the first skyscraper. Gilbert was a major figure in the development of the skyscraper, designing many tall buildings. His 60-storey Woolworth Building in New York City (1913) was the tallest building in the US at the time.

▶▶ The Father of Waters

The river Mississippi in North America, which rises in Minnesota near the Canadian border and flows south to a delta on the Gulf of Mexico, is known informally as the **Father of Waters**, with its chief tributary, the Missouri, regarded as its offspring. During the American Civil War, the Union forces under General Grant regained control of the Mississippi by beseiging the town of Vicksburg and eventually

capturing it on 4 July 1863. Abraham Lincoln was moved to
comment, 'the Father of Waters again goes unvexed to the sea.'

❯❯ Fats

Three rotund 20th-century musicians have been known as
Fats. The best known is probably Thomas **Fats** Waller
(1904–43), the US jazz pianist, composer, and singer. A
humorous and exuberant performer, his compositions include
'Ain't Misbehavin'' (1928) and 'Honeysuckle Rose' (1929).
Antoine **Fats** Domino (b.1928), the US singer, pianist, and
songwriter, wrote songs, such as 'Ain't That a Shame' (1955)
and 'Blueberry Hill' (1956), which marked the transition
from rhythm-and-blues to rock-and-roll. Domino's nickname
derived from his first commercial release in 1950, 'The Fat
Man'. The US bebop jazz trumpeter Theodore **Fats** Navarro
(1923–50) was called **Fat Girl** before becoming known as **Fats**
because of his size and high-pitched voice.

❯❯ Fatty

Roscoe **Fatty** Arbuckle (1887–1933) was an obese US
silent-film comedian. His film career was brought to an end
in 1921 by a scandal involving a wild party at which a starlet
called Virginia Rappe died. Arbuckle was charged with rape
and manslaughter and although he was later acquitted (after
three trials), he was shunned by movie audiences and his
films were banned. The nickname **Fatty Arbuckle** (or
sometimes **Fatty Harbuckle**) has subsequently been applied
to any portly person, often in the playground by children
who are unlikely ever to have heard of the actor.

❯❯ FDR

Franklin Delano Roosevelt (1882–1945) was the only US
President to be elected three times, and subsequently secured
a fourth term in office. His New Deal of 1933 helped to lift
the US out of the Great Depression, and he played an
important part in Allied policy during the Second World War.

His initials were used as a nickname, as with several other presidents.

›› Fiery Fred

The cricketer Fred Trueman (b.1931) was known as **Fiery Fred** because of his aggressive fast bowling for Yorkshire and England and his irascible manner. In 1964 he became the first bowler to take 300 test wickets, ending his test career with 307 wickets altogether.

›› The Fifth Beatle

A number of people have a claim to the title the **Fifth Beatle**. George Martin (b.1926) was a producer for the EMI Parlophone record label who worked with the Beatles on the arrangements of many of their songs and brought innovative four-track studio techniques to the recording of such albums as *Revolver* (1966) and *Sgt Pepper's Lonely Hearts Club Band* (1967). Brian Epstein (1934–67) first heard the Beatles play at the Cavern Club in Liverpool in 1961 and became their manager. He is credited with conceiving the band's image in its early years. Following Epstein's death by suicide in 1967, John Lennon said that they would not have made it without him. Yet another candidate for the title is Stuart Sutcliffe (1940–62), the band's original bass guitarist, who left the Beatles in 1961 and died the following year. Not only did the US musician Billy Preston (b.1946) play piano and organ on the *Let It Be* and *Abbey Road* albums, but the *Get Back* single is credited to 'The Beatles with Billy Preston', the first time another artist was so credited on a Beatles record.

›› The Fighting Boilermaker

When he started boxing professionally, Jim Jeffries (1875–1953) was known as the **Fighting Boilermaker** because he had earlier worked at the Lacey Manufacturing Company, a boiler-making factory near Los Angeles. He became world heavyweight champion in 1899, holding the title until his retirement in 1905. Jeffries was talked into making an ill-advised comeback six years later in an attempt to reclaim the title from the first black champion Jack Johnson.

❯❯ The Fighting Marine

Not long after turning professional, the boxer Gene Tunney (1897–1978) was drafted into the US Marine Corps. While stationed in France in 1919 he won the US Expeditionary Force's light-heavyweight championship. When he resumed his professional career he was therefore known as the **Fighting Marine**. Tunney beat Jack Dempsey in 1926 to become world heavyweight champion. He defended the title the following year against Dempsey in a famous fight that has become known as the 'Battle of the Long Count'.

❯❯ The First Gentleman of the Screen

After a distinguished stage career, the English actor George Arliss (1868–1946) became a film star in middle age. Suave and elegant on screen, he usually played monarchs, statesmen, millionaires, and the like, hence his nickname. He won an Oscar for *Disraeli* (1929), having previously played the part on stage in 1911 and in a silent film version in 1921.

❯❯ The First Lady of Hollywood

The Canadian film actress Norma Shearer (1900–83) was a major star of the 1920s and 30s, her films including *The Divorcee* (1930), for which she won an Oscar, and *Marie Antoinette* (1938). Shearer was dubbed both the **First Lady of Hollywood** and the **First Lady of the Screen**.

❯❯ The First State

The US state of Delaware is known as the **First State** because in 1787 it became the first state to ratify the new Constitution of the Union.

Film Stars

Ever since Clara Bow was dubbed the **It Girl** in the 1920s, Hollywood studios have promoted some of their female stars on the basis of their sex appeal:

the Anatomic Bomb — Silvana Pampanini
the Blonde Bombshell — Jean Harlow
the Body — Marie McDonald, Jamie Lee Curtis
the Girl with the Million Dollar Legs — Betty Grable
the Oomph Girl — Ann Sheridan
the Sweater Girl — Lana Turner

Some stars were given rather formal or aristocratic titles, often placing them at the top of their profession:

the Empress of Emotion — Elissa Landi
the First Gentleman of the Screen — George Arliss
the First Lady of Hollywood — Norma Shearer
the King of Hollywood — Clark Gable
the King of the Cowboys — Tom Mix, Roy Rogers
the Man of a Thousand Faces — Lon Chaney
the Man You Love to Hate — Erich von Stroheim

In some cases a film star's nickname reveals their country of origin or ethnic background:

the Austrian Oak —
   Arnold Schwarzenegger
the Brazilian Bombshell
   — Carmen Miranda
the Italian Stallion
   — Sylvester
   Stallone
**the Muscles from
   Brussels** — Jean-Claude Van Damme

▶▶ Flash Harry

Malcolm Sargent (1895–1967) was the conductor of the BBC
Symphony Orchestra (1950–57) and chief conductor of the
annual Promenade Concerts at London's Royal Albert Hall
(1957–67). He was known as **Flash Harry** because of his
dapper appearance and urbane charm. The term can be
generally applied to any extrovert and loudly-dressed show-
off or to someone with the air of a 'spiv'.

▶▶ The Flickertail State

The **Flickertail State** is the US state of North Dakota. A
flickertail is a popular name for Richardson's ground squirrel,
a burrowing rodent found in North Dakota.

▶▶ Flo-Jo

Florence Griffith-Joyner (1959–98) cut a glamorous figure in
the world of athletics, with her garishly coloured one-piece
bodysuits and her six-inch fingernails painted in rainbow
colours or in the Stars and Stripes. Widely known as **Flo-Jo**,
she won three gold medals at the 1988 Seoul Olympics (the
100m and 200m and the sprint relay). Her lucrative
sponsorship deals also earned her the nickname **Cash Flo**.

▶▶ The Floozie in the Jacuzzi

Birmingham's Victoria Square boasts a group of fountains
and cascades dominated by a massive sculpture of a female
figure in a pool. Weighing 1.75 tonnes, she represents the life
force. To local people she is affectionately known as the
Floozie in the Jacuzzi. This nickname is actually borrowed
from a sculpture that used to be situated in O'Connell St in
Dublin. A monument to Anna Livia, the personification of the
River Liffey, it represented the river as a female figure
reclining in a stream of bubbling water. Dubliners dubbed
this sculpture not only the Floozie in the Jacuzzi but also the
Hoor (that is, 'whore') **in the Sewer**.

›› Fluff

The disc jockey Alan Freeman (b.1927), whose career on British radio began in the early 1960s, has mainly worked for the BBC and Capital Radio. His catchphrases include 'Greetings, pop pickers!' and 'Not 'arf!'. Freeman's long-time nickname **Fluff** apparently comes from an old fluffy jumper that he once wore.

›› The Flying Dutchman

Baseball's **Flying Dutchman** was Honus Wagner (1874–1955), widely recognized as the greatest shortstop in the history of the game and an exceptional right-handed hitter. He was nicknamed after the legendary ghost ship *The Flying Dutchman* because of his Dutch ancestry and his tremendous speed as a base runner. Playing most of his career with the Pittsburgh Pirates, he stole over 20 bases every year from 1898 to 1915.

›› The Flying Dutchwoman

At the 1948 Olympics held in London, the Dutch athlete Fanny Blankers-Koen (1918–2004), a 30-year-old mother of two, was the oldest female competitor taking part in the Games. She caused a sensation by winning four gold medals, in the 100m, the 200m, the 80m hurdles, and the sprint relay. She was inevitably dubbed the **Flying Dutchwoman**, after the legendary ghost ship *The Flying Dutchman*. Another nickname was the **Flying Housewife**.

›› The Flying Finn

The Finnish athlete Paavo Nurmi (1897–1973) dominated middle- and long-distance running in the 1920s. Known for revolutionizing training methods, he won a total of nine Olympic gold medals, five of them at the 1924 Paris Olympics in the 1,500m, 3,000m steeplechase, 5,000m, and the cross-country team and individual events. Nurmi's alliterative nickname was the **Flying Finn** and the title has more recently been applied to the Finnish Formula One motor-racing driver Mika Hakkinen (b.1968), world champion in 1998 and 1999.

▶▶ The Flying Peacemaker

Henry Kissinger (b.1923), the German-born US statesman and diplomat, was Secretary of State 1973–77. In an era of shuttle diplomacy, Kissinger helped negotiate the withdrawal of US troops from South Vietnam, for which he shared the Nobel Peace Prize. He subsequently mediated between Israel and Syria in the wake of the Yom Kippur War.

▶▶ Foggy Bottom

The US State Department in Washington DC is often referred to as **Foggy Bottom**, from the traditional name of the swampy piece of land on which the office buildings were built. The term was first used in connection with the State Department by James Reston in the *New York Times* in 1947.

Football Clubs

The origins of football club nicknames fall into various categories, some of which are shown below, with examples of nicknames in each category.

Team strip:

the Bees — Barnet, Brentford
the Blues — Birmingham City, Chelsea, Manchester City
the Clarets — Burnley
the Magpies — Newcastle United, Notts County
the Reds — Barnsley, Liverpool, Nottingham Forest
the Robins — Cheltenham Town, Wrexham

Name of the stadium:

the Cottagers — Fulham (Craven Cottage)
the Merry Millers — Rotherham United (Millmoor)
the Owls — Sheffield United (formerly Owlerton, now
   Hillsborough)
the Shaymen — Halifax Town (The Shay)

Circumstances in which the club was founded:

the Gunners — Arsenal (formed by workers at the Royal Arsenal
   Armaments Factory in Woolwich in 1886)
the Hammers — West Ham United (formed in 1895 as the
   company team of the Thames Ironworks)
the Lions — Millwall (many of their early players were Scots and
   so the club adopted the lion on the Scottish flag for its badge)
the Posh — Peterborough United (when the club was formed in
   1934, the fans were promised 'posh players for a posh new
   team')

Local industry:

the Blades — Sheffield United (steel and cutlery)
the Canaries — Norwich City (breeding pet birds)
the Chairboys — Wycombe Wanderers (furniture-making)
the Cobblers — Northampton Town (shoe-making)
the Hatters — Luton Town (millinery)
the Mariners — Grimsby Town (fishing)
the Potters — Stoke City (pottery)

➤➤ The Forbidden City

Two cities are known as the **Forbidden City**, Lhasa and
Beijing. Lhasa, the capital of Tibet and the spiritual centre of
Tibetan Buddhism, was so-called because of its remoteness
and the fact that it was closed to foreign visitors until the
20th century. The name is also applied to a walled section of
Beijing, the capital of China, containing the former imperial
palaces, temples, and other buildings of the former Chinese
Empire. Entry was forbidden to all except the members of the
imperial family and their servants.

➤➤ The Forces' Sweetheart

During World War II Vera Lynn (b.1917) sang to British
servicemen, becoming known as the **Forces' Sweetheart**. She
is mainly remembered for such songs as 'We'll Meet Again'
and 'White Cliffs of Dover'. Her radio series *Sincerely Yours*
was aimed at the troops serving overseas. In 1975 she was
made a Dame.

➤➤ The Fordham Flash

In the 1920s and 30s Frankie Frisch (1898–1973) was a
baseball player with the New York Giants and St Louis
Cardinals. An outstanding fielder, his nickname the **Fordham
Flash** derived from his time as an undergraduate at Fordham
University, where he was an all-round sportsman.

➤➤ The Foxes

Leicester City football club was originally known as Leicester
Fosse because its founders' inaugural meeting in 1884 was
held at a house on the Fosse Way, an old Roman road. For
some years they were nicknamed the **Fossils**, but in 1919 the
club was renamed Leicester City and a new nickname was
adopted, the **Foxes**.

❯❯ Free-O

Free-O is the informal name for Fremantle, the principal port
of Western Australia, near the city of Perth. A refreshing sea
breeze that blows into Fremantle and Perth on warm
evenings is known locally as the **Fremantle Doctor**.

❯❯ The Free State

In 1923 Hamilton Owens, the editor of the *Baltimore Evening
Sun*, invented the name **Maryland Free State** to promote the
state's claim to be a sanctuary from the oppressive legislation
suffered by the rest of the country. The name caught on
within Maryland and was later shortened to the **Free State**.

❯❯ Frisco

The US city of San Francisco, California, is sometimes called
Frisco by non-residents, though the name is disliked by San
Franciscans themselves.

❯❯ Fritz

Walter Mondale (b.1928) served as Vice President under
Jimmy Carter 1977–81. Mondale was known as **Fritz**, from
his middle name Frederick. Fritz is the traditional short form
of the German name Friedrich.

▶▶ The Gabba

To cricket fans, the **Gabba** is the informal name for the Queensland Cricket Association's ground at Woollongabba, a suburb of Brisbane, Australia. A venue for Test matches, the **Gabba** is a shortening of Woollongabba.

▶▶ The Galloping Gourmet

In the late 1960s and early 1970s, the British television cook Graham Kerr (b.1934) was promoted as the **Galloping Gourmet** because of his frenetic style, dashing around the kitchen set as he prepared each dish.

▶▶ The Galloping Major

Ferenc Puskás (b.1927) was a key member of the great Hungarian national team of the early 1950s, playing in the stunning 6–3 victory over England at Wembley in 1952. In all Puskás played for Hungary 84 times, scoring 83 goals. In 1956 he left Hungary to play for Real Madrid, scoring four goals in their 1960 European Cup Final victory and a hat trick in the corresponding 1962 final, in which Real Madrid lost. Puskás was known as the **Galloping Major** because of his rank when he played for the Hungarian army club Honved.

▶▶ The Gamecock State

South Carolina's nickname the **Gamecock State** refers to the supposed belligerence of its inhabitants and in particular to its determined opposition to the abolition of slavery. A *gamecock* is a cock bred and trained for cockfighting. South Carolina was the first state to secede from the Union in 1860.

❯❯ The Gang of Four

In China, the **Gang of Four** was a group of four associates involved in implementing many of Mao Zedong's policies during the Cultural Revolution. The four members were Wang Hongwen, Zhang Chunjao, Yao Wenyuan, and Mao's wife Jiang Qing. They attempted to take power on Mao's death in 1976, but were arrested and imprisoned. In the UK, the name was applied to a group of four Labour MPs (Shirley Williams, Roy Jenkins, David Owen, and William Rodgers) who broke away from the Labour Party in 1981 to form the Social Democratic Party.

❯❯ The Garden of England

The **Garden of England** is the county of Kent, noted for its fertility and fruit-production. In the past the term was also applied to Worcestershire.

❯❯ The Garden State

As a producer of vegetables, fruit, and dairy products, the US state of New Jersey is known as the **Garden State**, though its economy is actually dominated by chemicals and pharmaceuticals manufacturing.

❯❯ Gaseous Cassius

Muhammad Ali. See ····➤ The **LOUISVILLE** Lip.

❯❯ Gazza

Paul Gascoigne's (b.1967) nickname **Gazza**, which the English footballer had acquired at the age of 12, caught on to such an extent that it was registered as a trademark by his agent and it inspired a succession of similar '-zza' coinages. For example, the politicians Michael Heseltine and John Prescott became known as **Hezza** and **Prezza** respectively. During England's World Cup semi-final with West Germany in 1990, Gascoigne received a second yellow card which would have ruled him out of the final, had England beaten West Germany. His tearful reaction endeared him to the British public and he became a hugely popular national figure overnight. After Gascoigne transferred from Tottenham Hotspur to the Italian club Lazio the Italian fans continued to call him **Gazza** ('magpie' in Italian), coincidentally appropriate for a player who had previously played for Newcastle United (nicknamed the **Magpies**).

➤➤ The Gem State

The name of Idaho, the US state, is popularly though mistakenly supposed to come from an Indian word meaning 'mountain gem', hence the state's nickname the **Gem State**.

➤➤ George Cross Island

An important British naval base in the Mediterranean in the Second World War, the island of Malta sustained heavy Italian and German air attack between 1940 and 1942, throughout which the people of the island put up steadfast resistance. In April 1942 George VI awarded the island the George Cross, a British medal given to civilians for courage in circumstances of extreme danger, in recognition of the bravery and endurance of its inhabitants. Malta duly became known as **George Cross Island** and a representation of the medal appears on the Maltese flag.

➤➤ The Georgia Peach

Ty Cobb (1886–1961) is widely acclaimed as one of the greatest players in the history of baseball. The Georgia-born Cobb holds the record for runs scored (2,254) and lifetime

batting average (0.367), and became the first player elected
to baseball's Hall of Fame in 1936. His career total of 4,191
hits was a major league record for almost 60 years. Georgia is
itself known as the **Peach State**.

▶▶ The Gherkin

The **Gherkin** is the popular nickname of the Swiss Re
building at 30 Saint Mary Axe, London. Completed in 2004,
this 40-floor office tower built by the architect Norman Foster
for the financial services group Swiss Reinsurance is 590ft
(180m) tall. The distinctive shape of the cylindrical tower,
which tapers towards the top and is capped by a rounded
cone, has led Londoners to also call it the **Erotic Gherkin** and
the **Towering Innuendo**.

▶▶ The Gipper

As US president, Ronald Reagan (b.1911) used to tell his
supporters to 'win one for the Gipper'. A former film actor,
Reagan appeared in the 1940 film *Knute Rockne — All
American* in the role of the real-life American footballer
George Gipp (1895–1920). Nicknamed the **Gipper**, Gipp died
young from pneumonia. On his deathbed he said to Knute
Rockne, his team's coach, 'Someday, when things look real
tough for Notre Dame, ask the boys to go out there and win
one for the Gipper.'

▶▶ The Girl with the Million Dollar Legs

Betty Grable (1916–73) starred in such Hollywood comedies
and musicals as *Million Dollar Legs* (1939) and *Pin Up Girl*
(1944). Her shapely legs were reportedly insured for a
million dollars (in fact $250,000) with Lloyds of London.
Grable herself said: 'There are two reasons why I'm in show
business, and I'm standing on both of them'. A picture of her
wearing a white bathing suit made her the most popular pin-
up of the Second World War.

>> Give 'Em Hell Harry

Harry S. Truman (1884–1972) became US president on the
death of Franklin Roosevelt in 1945. He went on to fight and
win the election of 1948. During the presidential campaign
he told his running mate Alben W. Barkley, 'I'm going to fight
hard. I'm going to give 'em hell.' Suiting his combative
personality, **Give 'Em Hell Harry** became his nickname,
though he later said in an interview, 'I never give them hell. I
just tell the truth. And they think it is hell.'

>> The Glaziers

Crystal Palace football club was named after the Crystal
Palace, originally built in 1851 to house the Great Exhibition
in Hyde Park and moved to Sydenham Hill in South London
soon afterwards. They were nicknamed the **Glaziers** after this
enormous glass-and-iron structure. In the 1970s the club
dropped their old nickname in favour of the **Eagles**.

>> The Gloomy Dean

The **Gloomy Dean** was William Ralph Inge (1860–1954), the
English theologian and dean of St Paul's Cathedral 1911–34.
He wrote a column for the London *Evening Standard* in the
1930s, his nickname coming from his pessimistic outlook on
numerous political and social issues.

>> The Gloved One

Pop star Michael Jackson (b.1958) was known as the **Gloved
One** at the height of his success in the 1980s. This was
because of the single white sequined glove that became his
visual trademark.

>> The Gnome

Keith Fletcher (b.1944), the Essex and England cricketer,
was nicknamed the **Gnome**, partly from his slight

appearance and partly from his somewhat hunched, introspective style of batting.

>> The Goat

The **Goat** was one of the nicknames of David Lloyd George (1863–1945), the British Prime Minister 1916–22. Referring to his lecherous reputation and extra-marital affairs, the subject of much gossip, it was coined by a senior civil servant Robert Chalmers when Lloyd George was Chancellor of the Exchequer.

>> The Godfather of Soul

James Brown (b.1928), the pioneering soul and funk singer and songwriter, first started calling himself the **Godfather of Soul** in the 1970s. His many soul hits include 'Papa's Got a Brand New Bag' (1965), 'I Got You (I Feel Good)' (1965), and 'Sex Machine' (1970). Brown's other nicknames include the **Hardest Working Man in Show Business** and **Mr Dynamite**.

>> God's Banker

Roberto Calvi (1920–82) was known as **God's Banker** because the Italian banker had close links to the Vatican. In 1982 Calvi was found hanging under Blackfriars Bridge in London, his pockets weighted down with bricks. Although his death was initially treated by British police as suicide, later evidence suggested that Calvi was probably murdered by the Mafia.

>> The Gold Coast

The **Gold Coast** is the name for an affluent residential area along Lake Shore Drive in Chicago, bordering Lake Michigan. It comprises luxurious hotels, private mansions, and high-rise apartment houses. The **Gold Coast** was the former name (until 1957) for Ghana in West Africa, so called because it was an important source of gold.

›› Goldenballs

In September 2001 Victoria Beckham revealed on the
Parkinson TV chat show that her own nickname for her
husband, the English footballer David Beckham (b.1975),
was **Goldenballs**. This was enthusiastically taken up by the
press.

›› The Golden Bear

The US golfer Jack Nicklaus (b.1940) is often regarded as the
greatest player ever. He won 18 professional major
championships, including six wins in the Masters, five in the
PGA, four in the US Open, and three in the British Open. He
was nicknamed the **Golden Bear** because of his sturdy build
and blond hair.

›› The Golden Boy

Two pop singers were dubbed the **Golden Boy**, Frankie
Avalon and Paul Anka. Frankie Avalon (b.1939) was a US
teen idol of the 1950s, successful both as a pop singer and a
film actor, especially in a series of beach movies. His hits
included 'Venus' (1959) and 'Why' (1959). Paul Anka
(b.1941) was a Canadian pop singer, known for such songs
as 'Diana' and for writing the English lyrics of the French
singer-songwriter Claude François's song 'My Way'. A cinema
short about Anka, released in 1962, had the title *Golden Boy*.
The term was originally the title of a play by Clifford Odets
(1937), later filmed. It can be applied to any popular,
talented, or successful young man.

›› The Golden Foghorn

The **Golden Foghorn** was Ethel Merman (1909–84), the
US musical comedy star with a dynamic personality and an
ear-splitting voice. She starred in such Broadway shows as
Annie Get Your Gun (1946), *Call Me Madam* (1950), and

Gypsy (1958). The first of these contained one of the songs with which she is most associated, 'There's No Business Like Show Business'.

▶▶ The Golden Gate City

The US city of San Francisco, California, is sometimes called the **Golden Gate City**. The Golden Gate is the mile-wide strait connecting San Francisco Bay with the Pacific Ocean. It is spanned by the Golden Gate single-span suspension bridge (completed 1937).

▶▶ The Golden State

The **Golden State** is Calfornia. The nickname originally referred to the discovery of gold in the Sierra Nevada in 1848, which led to the gold rush of 1849–56. Later the name was taken to be a reference to California's sunshine. California's state flower is the Golden Poppy.

▶▶ The Goober State

Famous for its peanut farming, the US state of Georgia is known as the **Goober State**. *Goober* is a 19th-century Southern US word for a peanut, ultimately of Bantu origin.

▶▶ *Goodtime George*

George Melly (b.1926), the English jazz singer, writer, and bon viveur, is nicknamed **Goodtime George**. This comes from John Chiltern's song of that title, which Melly regularly performs.

▶▶ *GOP*

The US Republican Party. See ⋯▶ The **GRAND** Old Party.

▶▶ The Gopher State

A Gopher is an informal term for a native or inhabitant of the US state of Minnesota, with reference to the burrowing rodent of the same name. Minnesota's nickname the **Gopher State** dates back to the late part of the 19th century.

▶▶ Gorbals Mick

The Scottish MP Michael Martin (b.1945) became Speaker of the House of Commons in 2000. His heavy Glasgow accent and working-class origins as a former sheetmetal worker prompted the London-based press to poke fun at Martin by calling him **Gorbals Mick**. The Gorbals is a working-class district of Glasgow, once known for its slums.

▶▶ Gorby

Mikhail Gorbachev (b.1931) was leader of the Soviet Union from 1985 until 1991. His foreign policy brought about an end to the cold war, while within the USSR he introduced major reforms known as *glasnost* 'being public' and *perestroika* 'reconstructing'. Hugely popular in the West in the late 1980s, Gorbachev was affectionately nicknamed **Gorby** in the press and the term Gorbymania was used to describe the enthusiastic public reaction to his visits abroad.

▶▶ Gorgeous George

The US professional wrestler George Wagner (1915–63), a master of self-promotion, called himself **Gorgeous George**. He had long curly hair dyed platinum blond and wore elaborate robes to enter the ring. The name Gorgeous George was supposedly first shouted at him by female spectators.

▶▶ Gorgeous Gussie

Gussie Moran (b.1923), the US tennis player, caused a sensation at Wimbledon in 1949 by wearing frilly lace panties under her tennis dress, designed by the ex-player and fashion designer Teddy Tinling (1910–90). Although hugely popular with the public, she was accused by the Wimbledon authorities of 'bringing vulgarity and sin into tennis'.

›› Gotham

New York City's nickname **Gotham** was coined by
Washington Irving in *Salmagundi* (1807). It refers to a village
in Nottinghamshire associated with the English folk tale 'The
Wise Men of Gotham', in which the villagers demonstrated
cunning by pretending to be stupid. The fictional Gotham
City, based on New York, is the setting of the Batman stories.

›› The Governator

Arnold Schwarzenegger (b.1947), the Austrian-born US movie
star, was elected governor of California in October 2003.
During his election campaign he was dubbed the **Governator**, a
blend of *governor* and *The Terminator*, the title of the 1984 film
in which he played an almost indestructible and emotionless
android. When allegations about Schwarzenegger's past,
particularly claims of sexual misconduct and pro-Nazi beliefs,
failed to stick to the candidate, he was also hailed as the **Teflon
Terminator**. Another nickname was **Conan the Republican**,
combining a reference to his 1982 film *Conan the Barbarian*
with a nod to his political affiliations.

5. *The Governator*

➤➤ The Gov'nor

Frank Sinatra. See ····➤ The **CHAIRMAN** of the Board.

➤➤ The Grand Canyon State

The **Grand Canyon State** is the official nickname of Arizona and appears on licence plates. The Grand Canyon is a deep gorge in Arizona, formed by the Colorado River, which is about 440km (277 miles) long, 8 to 24km (5 to 15 miles) wide, and, in places, 1,800m (6,000ft) deep.

➤➤ Grandma Moses

Grandma Moses is the name by which the self-taught US primitive painter Anna Mary Moses (1860–1961) is generally known. She did not begin to paint until she was nearly 70, going on to produce more than a thousand paintings in naive style, mostly of rural life in New England. Grandma Moses was still painting at the age of 100.

➤➤ The Grand Old Party

In the US, the Republican Party is known as the **Grand Old Party** , a term recorded from the late 19th century. It is sometimes abbreviated to **GOP**.

➤➤ The Granite City

The Scottish city of Aberdeen is nicknamed the **Granite City** on account of the local granite used in many of its public buildings.

➤➤ The Granite State

New Hampshire's nickname is the **Granite State** because the state's mountain region is composed mainly of granite, the quarrying of which was once a major industry.

›› Grandpa England

Grandpa England is how George V's (1865–1936)
granddaughters, the Princesses Elizabeth and Margaret, are
said to have referred to him when they were children.

›› The Grauniad

The Guardian newspaper is affectionately known as the
Grauniad (an anagram of its name) because of its reputation
for misprints. The nickname was coined in the 1970s by the
satirical magazine *Private Eye*.

›› The Great Communicator

US president Ronald Reagan (1911–2004) was immensely
popular with the American public. His background as a
film actor could be seen in the folksy, conversational
delivery of his speeches and in his skilful use of television
and radio. He therefore became known as the **Great
Communicator**.

›› The Greatest

Even before he won the gold medal in the 1960 Olympic
Games, the boxer Cassius Clay, later to change his name to
Muhammad Ali (b.1942), was bragging 'I'll be the greatest of
all time'. After he defeated Sonny Liston in 1964 to become
world champion, he shouted to the press: 'I told you, I told
you, I AM the Greatest!' He later revealed that he borrowed
his catchphrase from a wrestler called Gorgeous George
(born George Raymond Wagner), who promoted himself with
similar swagger.

›› The Great Lake State

Michigan state is comprised of two peninsulas in the midst of
the Great Lakes and divided by Lake Michigan, hence its
nickname the **Great Lake State**. The Great Lakes, a group of

five connected freshwater lakes along the US–Canada border, are made up of Lakes Superior, Michigan, Huron, Erie, and Ontario.

▸▸ The Great Lover

Two screen actors have laid claim to the title the **Great Lover**, Rudolph Valentino and Charles Boyer. Rudolph Valentino (1895–1926) became a leading star of silent films in the 1920s, playing the archetypal romantic lover in films such as *The Sheikh* (1921) and *Blood and Sand* (1922). He was one of the screen's first sex symbols. After Valentino's sudden death from peritonitis his funeral resulted in scenes of mass hysteria. The French-born US actor Charles Boyer (1897–1977) played romantic leading roles in films such as *Mayerling* (1936).

▸▸ The Great One

The Canadian ice-hockey player Wayne Gretzky (b.1961) is often considered the sport's best ever player, hence his emphatic nickname the **Great One**. He played with the Edmonton Oilers 1979–88 and with the Los Angeles Kings from 1988. Gretzky holds the records for the most goals scored in a season (92, in 1981–82) and the most career points.

▸▸ The Great Profile

John Barrymore (1882–1942) was both a distinguished stage actor, celebrated for his Hamlet (1922), and a flamboyant matinee idol, starring in such films as *Don Juan* (1926), *Grand Hotel* (1932), *Dinner at Eight* (1933), and *Twentieth Century* (1934). His handsome looks and aquiline nose earned him the nickname the **Great Profile** or simply the **Profile**.

▸▸ The Great White Hope

When Jack Johnson (1878–1946) knocked out Tommy Burns to become the first black heavyweight champion in 1908, many white American boxing fans looked for a **Great White Hope** to win it back. Stanley Ketchel was Johnson's first challenger in 1909. James J. Jeffries, who had retired in 1905, was talked into making a comeback six years later to take on the champion Johnson in Reno, Nevada. Billed as the 'Battle of the Century' and taking place in front of a racially hostile crowd, the contest was a one-sided affair won by the champion. Johnson had three further successful defences. Finally in 1915 Jess Willard (1883–1968), from Pottawatomie County, Kansas, challenged Johnson in Havana, Cuba. Also known as **Cowboy Jess** and the **Pottawatomie Giant** (he was over 6½ ft (198cm) tall), Willard won by a knockout in the 26th round. Many have suspected that the fight was fixed. Nearly 70 years later the title **Great White Hope** was revived for Gerry Cooney (b.1956) when he unsuccessfully challenged Larry Holmes in a highly publicized fight for the WBC heavyweight title in 1982.

⟫ The Great White Shark

The Australian golfer Greg Norman (b.1955) was one of the world's leading players in the 1980s and 1990s. He won the world matchplay championship three times (1980, 1983, 1986) and the British Open twice (1986, 1993). The blond-haired Norman became known as the **Great White Shark** or the **White Shark** because he used to fish for shark off the Brisbane coast. The name was apparently coined in 1981 by a newspaper in Augusta, Georgia, following an interview Norman gave during the US Masters. Norman now presides over a multinational business, involved in such activities as golf course design and property development, called Great White Shark Enterprises.

⟫ The Great White Way

New York City's **Great White Way** is Broadway, especially the part that runs between 41st and 53rd Streets. The nickname refers to the brilliant illumination used for theatres, cinemas, clubs, and advertising signs. It is the title of a novel written by Albert Bigelow Paine in 1901.

❯❯ The Green Goddess

In the 1980s, a familiar figure on BBC breakfast television was the keep-fit demonstrator Diana Moran (b.1940). She was billed as the **Green Goddess** because of the green catsuit she wore. The original Green Goddess was a green-painted military fire engine first used during the Second World War.

❯❯ The Green Mountain State

The US state of Vermont takes its nickname the **Green Mountain State** from the Green Mountains, a range in the northern Appalachians covered with evergreen forests. The name Vermont itself comes from the French *vert mont*, 'green mountain'.

❯❯ Grim Grom

Andrei Gromyko (1909–89) was Foreign Minister of the USSR 1957–85 and President 1985–88. His dour demeanour when conducting diplomatic negotiations during his 28 years as foreign minister earned him the press nickname **Grim Grom**.

❯❯ The Grinder

The Canadian snooker player Cliff Thorburn (b.1948), who won the World Professional championship in 1980, was known by his fellow-players as the **Grinder** because of his success in wearing down his opponents over the course of a match and his stubborn refusal to consider himself beaten.

❯❯ The Grocer

The satirical magazine *Private Eye* called Edward Heath (b.1916) the **Grocer**, a reference to his role as chief negotiator for British entry into the Common Market in 1961–62, when much of his time was spent haggling over the price of hundreds of foodstuffs. During Heath's time as prime minister, the magazine featured a cartoon strip called 'Grocer Heath and His Pals'.

›› The Grocer's Daughter

While Margaret Thatcher (b.1925) was indeed the daughter of a Grantham grocer, her nickname the **Grocer's Daughter** was apt for another reason. Her predecessor as leader of the Conservative Party was Edward Heath, known as the **Grocer**.

›› The Guinea Pig State

The US state of Arkansas earned its nickname the **Guinea Pig State** in the 1930s when its farmers volunteered to take part in the agricultural experiments suggested by the federal government.

›› The Gunners

Arsenal football club was formed by workers at the Royal Arsenal Armaments Factory in Woolwich in 1886, hence the club nickname the **Gunners**.

›› Guy the Gorilla

English cricketer Ian Botham (b.1955) was known as **Guy the Gorilla** because of his powerful build. The original Guy was a gorilla that used to be a popular attraction at London Zoo.

›› The Hags with the Bags

Near to the Ha'penny Bridge in Dublin is a sculpture of two women chatting on a bench with their shopping bags by their feet. This is known locally as the **Hags with the Bags**.

›› The Hammer

David McNee (b.1925) served as Commissioner of the Metropolitan Police from 1977 to 1982. He had earlier gained both a reputation for toughness and his nickname the **Hammer** from his robust approach to law and order while serving as Chief Constable of Glasgow (1971–75).

›› Hammerin' Hank

The baseball player Hank Aaron (b.1934) was known as **Hammerin' Hank**. In 1973 he overtook Babe Ruth's record of 714 career home runs, ending his career with total of 755. When he broke Ruth's legendary record (which had stood since 1935) Aaron was the object of racist abuse from many resentful baseball fans.

›› The Hammers

West Ham United football club was formed in 1895 as the company team of the Thames Ironworks, hence their nickname the **Hammers**, or, formerly, the **Irons**.

›› The Handcuff King

The **Handcuff King** was how Harry Houdini (1874–1926), the Hungarian-born US magician and escape artist, used to be billed. In the early 1900s he became famous for his ability to escape from handcuffs and chains, from straitjackets, from locked containers, and from prison cells.

›› The Hanging State

In 1975, the Australian state of Victoria became the last state in the country to abolish capital punishment, hence its nickname the **Hanging State**.

›› Hands of Stone

Born in Panama, the boxer Roberto Duran (b.1951) was a ferocious puncher known as *Manos de Piedra* or **Hands of Stone**. In the 1970s and 80s he was world champion at lightweight, welterweight, super-welterweight, and middleweight.

›› The Hangman of Europe

As second-in-command of the Gestapo and head of the security service, Reinhard Heydrich (1904–42) was responsible for ordering numerous mass executions in the occupied countries, hence his nickname the **Hangman of Europe**. He was assassinated by Czech patriots, reprisals for which included the execution of 1,300 civilian inhabitants of the village of Lidice.

›› Hanoi Jane

The US film actress Jane Fonda (b.1937) campaigned against American involvement in the Vietnam War, and in 1972 made a trip to Hanoi to denounce the US bombing campaigns against North Vietnam. During this visit she volunteered to make a number of propaganda broadcasts

over Radio Hanoi intended to demoralize US servicemen.
This made her unpopular with many Americans at the time:
the disapproving nickname **Hanoi Jane** was consciously
modelled on that of ····➤ TOKYO Rose, notorious for
broadcasting propaganda to GIs from Japan during the
Second World War.

▶▶ The Hatters

Luton Town football club are known as the **Hatters**, from the
town's once-thriving millinery industry, especially the
manufacture of straw hats.

▶▶ Hawk

Coleman Hawkins. See ····➤ BEAN.

▶▶ The Hawkeye State

Iowa's nickname the **Hawkeye State** is first recorded around
1859. The informal term Hawkeye for a native of Iowa may
have originated with the newspaper editor J. G. Edwards
who was the editor of the Burlington *Patriot* and himself
nicknamed **Old Hawkeye**. The newsaper was later retitled the
Hawkeye and Patriot.

▶▶ The Head Waiter

The British jockey Harry Wragg (1902–85) won the Derby in
1928, 1930, and 1942, and rode another ten classic winners.
Wragg was champion jockey in 1941. His nickname the **Head
Waiter** refers to his tactic of waiting until the very end of a
race before taking the front and crossing the line first.

▶▶ The Heart of Dixie

The **Heart of Dixie** is the US state of Alabama. Dixie is an
informal name for the Southern states of the US. The
origin of the term is not entirely certain, although it has

been suggested that the name comes from French *dix* 'ten' on ten-dollar notes printed before the Civil War by the Citizens Bank of Louisiana, and circulating in the Southern states.

❯❯ Heff

In 1953 Hugh Hefner (b.1926), informally known as **Heff**, founded *Playboy*, an erotic magazine for men. He later set up the Playboy chain of nightclubs, whose 'Bunny girl' hostesses wore skimpy costumes with a rabbit's ears and tail.

❯❯ Hell's Kitchen

Hell's Kitchen is a district on the West Side of New York City once regarded as the haunt of criminals. The term can be applied to any area or place regarded as very disreputable or unpleasant.

❯❯ The Herring Pond

First recorded in the late 17th century, the **Herring Pond** (or the **Pond**) is a humorous nickname for the North Atlantic.

❯❯ Hezza

The Conservative politician Michael Heseltine (b.1933) was known as **Hezza**, an echo of the footballer Paul Gascoigne's nickname ••••➤ GAZZA. Heseltine mentions in his autobiography that it is said to have been invented by Alastair Campbell when he was a journalist, before he became Tony Blair's press secretary.

❯❯ The Hill

Washington's Capitol Hill, informally known as the **Hill**, is where the Congress buildings and Supreme Court stand. By extension, the term can be used to refer to Congress itself.

›› His Royal Badness

In 1993 the rock musician Prince (born Prince Rogers Nelson) (b.1958) announced that he had changed his name to an unpronounceable symbol and should thereafter be referred to as 'the Artist formerly known as Prince'. Earlier in his career he had been known both as **His Royal Badness** and as the **Purple Pixie**, from his preference for dressing in purple and his short stature.

›› Hitch

The English film director Alfred Hitchcock (1899–1980), informally known as **Hitch**, became best known for such thrillers as *Strangers on a Train* (1951), *North by Northwest* (1959), *Psycho* (1960), and *The Birds* (1963). These films are notable for their ability to generate suspense and for their technical ingenuity. He was billed on film posters as the **Master of Suspense**.

›› Hit 'em Where They Ain't

Willie Keeler (1872–1923), the US baseball player, mostly played with the Baltimore Orioles and New York Yankees (1892–1910). His nickname comes from his own summary of his batting style: 'Keep your eye on the ball and hit 'em where they ain't'. Only 5ft 4in (1.64m), he was also known as **Wee Willie**.

›› The Hit Man

Thomas Hearns (b.1958) was the first boxer to win championships at five different weights: welterweight, light-middleweight, middleweight, light-heavyweight, and super-middleweight. Hearns was an explosive puncher, hence his nickname the **Hit Man**.

›› The Hog and Hominy State

Tennessee's nickname the **Hog and Hominy State** refers to the traditional local diet of fatback pork and cornmeal.

›› Hollywood

The Australian leg-spin bowler Shane Warne (b.1969) is his country's highest-ever wicket-taker in Test matches. His nickname **Hollywood** was coined by the Australian Rules footballer Trevor Barker in the early days of Warne's career and comes from the cricketer's superstar image and the amount of press attention he attracts. Teammates also call him **Truman**, after the film *The Truman Show*, starring Jim Carrey, in which a man's life is filmed 24 hours a day for a television show. Another of Warne's nicknames is the **Sultan of Spin**.

›› Hollywood's Mermaid

The former swimming champion Esther Williams (b.1923) made her film debut in 1942. She went on to appear in a series of MGM musicals whose spectacular aquatic sequences made full use of her superb swimming ability, among them *Bathing Beauty* (1944), *Neptune's Daughter* (1949), *Million Dollar Mermaid* (1952), and *Dangerous When Wet* (1953). In the memorable words of producer Joe Pasternak, 'Wet she was a star'.

›› Homicide Hank

Henry Armstrong (1912–88), or **Homicide Hank**, is the only boxer to have held three world titles simultaneously, namely featherweight, lightweight, and welterweight. He was also known as **Hurricane Hank** and the **Human Buzzsaw**, because of the speed and ferocity with which he assaulted his opponents.

›› Honkers

From the 1920s the former British colony of Hong Kong was informally known as **Honkers** by British expatriates living and working there.

›› The Hoosier State

A Hoosier is a native or inhabitant of Indiana. The term, dating from around 1826, is of unknown origin. Around the same time Indiana began to be referred to as the **Hoosier State**.

›› Hunt the Shunt

British motor-racing driver James Hunt (1947–93) won the World Motor-racing Championship in 1976 by one point. In his early years of racing Minis and in Formula Three, he became saddled with the tag **Hunt the Shunt** because of the number of crashes he was involved in.

›› Hurricane

Alex Higgins (b.1949), the Northern Irish snooker player, won the World Professional snooker championship in 1972 and 1982. His first manager John McLaughlin gave him his nickname **Hurricane Higgins**, which well suited his quick-fire style of play.

›› Hurricane Hank

Henry Armstrong. See ····➤ **HOMICIDE** Hank.

>> Ian Macabre

Ian McEwan (b.1948) is an English writer whose novels include *The Child in Time* (1987), *Enduring Love* (1997), and *Atonement* (2001). Because his early collections of short stories, *First Love, Last Rites* (1975) and *In Between the Sheets* (1977), were characterized by an interest in violence, sexual perversion, and obsession, he attracted for a time the tag **Ian Macabre**.

>> Iceberg[1]

In the 1950s Grace Kelly (1928–82) starred in such films as *High Noon* (1952), *Rear Window (1954), Dial M for Murder* (1954), and *High Society* (1955). A cool blonde beauty, she projected an aloof presence on screen and, according to some of her co-stars, on set too. This is why she was dubbed **Iceberg**, the **Ice Princess**, and **Fair Miss Frigidaire**, this last coined by Frank Sinatra. Kelly retired from her film career in 1956 to marry Prince Rainier III of Monaco. She died in 1982 in a road accident.

>> The Iceberg[2]

Björn Borg (b.1956), the Swedish tennis player, won five consecutive men's singles titles at Wimbledon (1976–80) and six French Open singles titles (1974–75 and 1978–81). Borg's cool, undemonstrative demeanour on court led the press to call him the **Iceberg**, or, echoing his surname, the **Iceborg**.

➤➤ IDS

Iain Duncan Smith (b.1954) was leader of the Conservative
Party 2001–03, during which time he was informally known
as **IDS**, a nickname supposed to echo those of the US
presidents FDR, JFK, and LBJ. In October 2003, on the eve of
the leadership contest which was to see Duncan Smith
replaced by Michael Howard, the *Sun* carried the witty
headline 'Adios IDS'.

➤➤ Ike

Dwight Eisenhower (1890–1969) was the Allied commander
in Europe during the Second World War and later president of
the US 1953–61. **Ike** was a childhood nickname, derived from
his surname, which he carried into adult life. It caught on with
the American public in the form of the slogan 'I Like Ike', used
in Eisenhower's presidential campaigns of 1952 and 1956,
though the phrase was used as early as 1947 when he was first
being talked about as a possible presidential candidate.

➤➤ The In and Out

94 Piccadilly in London used to be home to the Naval and
Military Club, founded in 1862. The club's nickname the **In
and Out** refers to the words 'In' and 'Out' that were painted in
bold lettering on the gateposts flanking the approach to the
courtyard, and is thought to have originated with London
cabbies. The club moved to new premises in St James's
Square in 1998.

➤➤ The Iron

Scunthorpe United football club's nickname the **Iron** stems
from the town's steel mills.

➤➤ The Iron Butterfly

In the 1930s Jeanette Macdonald (1901–65) appeared with

Nelson Eddy (1901–67) in an immensely popular series of film operettas, such as *Naughty Marietta* (1935) and *Rose Marie* (1936). Probably the most successful singing duo in the history of cinema, the pair were unkindly nicknamed the **Iron Butterfly** and the **Singing Capon**.

➤➤ The Iron Chancellor

Gordon Brown (b.1951) has been British Chancellor of the Exchequer since 1997. In May 1995, while still in Opposition, Brown promised to be an **Iron Chancellor** if Labour were elected: 'Nobody should doubt my iron commitment to macroeconomic stability and financial prudence.' Brown was deliberately echoing the phrase associated with Otto von Bismarck (1815–98), Chancellor of the German Empire 1871–90. Bismarck was nicknamed the **Iron Chancellor** after he used the phrase 'blood and iron' in a speech to the Prussian parliament in 1862, referring to military force as an instrument of foreign policy.

➤➤ Iron City

The US city of Pittsburgh, Pennsylvania, is known as the **Iron City**. Following the discovery of iron deposits and rich coalfields, Pittsburgh, with its large steel mills, was for a century (until the 1980s) a centre of iron and steel production in the US.

➤➤ The Iron Horse

In his 17-year baseball career, Lou Gehrig (1903–41) played 2,130 consecutive major-league games for the New York Yankees (1925–39), a record games-played streak that was finally beaten in 1995 by Carl Ripken. Gehrig's great stamina earned him his nickname the **Iron Horse**. He died aged 38 from a form of motor neuron disease now often called Lou Gehrig's disease.

6. *Margaret Thatcher as the Iron Lady, January 1976*

➤➤ The Iron Lady

In January 1976, before she became prime minister, Margaret Thatcher (b.1925) was dubbed the **Iron Lady** by the Soviet defence ministry newspaper *Red Star*, which accused her of trying to revive the Cold War. She immediately responded to the name: 'I stand before you tonight in my red chiffon evening gown, my face softly made up, my fair hair gently waved...the Iron Lady of the Western World! Me? A cold war warrior? Well, yes—if that is how they wish to interpret my defence of values and freedoms fundamental to our way of life.'

➤➤ The Iron Man

The Czech athlete Emil Zatopek (1922–2000) was the greatest long-distance runner of his day, known for his head-rolling style of running and the contorted expression on his face. He won the 10,000m at the 1948 Olympics and four years later won gold medals in the 5,000m, 10,000m, and the marathon. Zatopek was known as the **Iron Man** because of his strength and endurance.

›› Iron Mike

When the boxer Mike Tyson (b.1966) won the WBC heavyweight title in 1986, he became the youngest world heavyweight champion ever. The following year he became the first undisputed world heavyweight champion since 1978, having won the WBC, WBA, and IBF titles. An intimidating, seemingly indestructible boxer, he was known simply as **Iron Mike**. In 1992 Tyson was imprisoned for rape and was referred to during his four years of incarceration as **Leg Iron Mike**.

›› The Italian Stallion

The **Italian Stallion** was the nickname of Rocky Balboa, the Italian-American boxer played by Sylvester Stallone (b.1946) in *Rocky* (1976), the film that made Stallone's name, and in a number of sequels. The nickname subsequently transferred to the actor himself, who is also familiarly known as **Sly**.

›› The It Girl

The US film actress Clara Bow (1905–65) was one of the most popular stars and sex-symbols of the 1920s. She became known as the **It Girl** after appearing as a vivacious flapper in the silent film *It* (1927), based on an Elinor Glyn novel. The word 'it' here means sex appeal. She once said: 'Being a sex-symbol is a heavy load to carry, especially when one is tired, hurt and bewildered'.

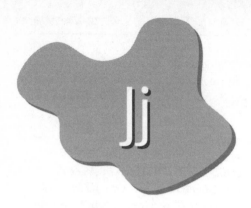

▶▶ The Jackal

The **Jackal** was the name journalists gave to Carlos Martinez (b.1949), a Venezuelan assassin hired by various terrorist organizations in the 1970s. It was taken from the codename used by the professional assassin in Frederick Forsyth's thriller *The Day of the Jackal* (1971), about a plot to kill President de Gaulle.

▶▶ Jackie O

Jacqueline Kennedy (1929–94) was a popular and glamorous First Lady before her husband President John F. Kennedy's assassination in 1963. Following her subsequent marriage to the Greek shipping magnate and financier Aristotle Onassis (1906–75), she became known as **Jackie O** (short for Onassis), before being widowed for a second time in 1975.

▶▶ Jacko

Michael Jackson (b.1958), informally known as **Jacko**, was the most commercially successful US pop star of the 1980s. His albums include *Thriller* (1982), *Bad* (1987), and *Dangerous* (1991). Accounts of his eccentric behaviour have led newspapers to dub him **Wacko** and **Wacko Jacko**. There has been a good deal of speculation about the singer's appearance. Jackson himself attributes the lightening of his skin to a rare skin disorder and has repeatedly denied undergoing plastic surgery to change the shape of his face.

Jazz Musicians

Jazz is well-stocked with colourful nicknames. The ranks of jazz
nobility include a **King** (Oliver), a **Duke** (Ellington), a **Count**
(Basie) and a **Baron** (Lee). There is also an **Earl** (Hines),
although he was actually born with that name. And Billie
Holiday was known as **Lady Day**.

Some of the other jazz nicknames explained in these pages
are:

Bean — Coleman Hawkins
Bird — Charlie Parker
Chu — Leon Berry
Dippermouth — Louis Armstrong
Dizzy Gillespie
Fatha — Earl Hines
Hawk — Coleman Hawkins
Jelly Roll Morton
The Lion — Willie Smith
Pops — Louis Armstrong,
Paul Whiteman
Prez — Lester Young
Rabbit — Jonny Hodges
Satchmo — Louis
Armstrong
Smack — Fletcher Henderson
Swee' Pea — Billy Strayhorn
Trane — John Coltrane
Yardbird — Charlie Parker
Zoot Sims

❯❯ Jack the Dripper

The US painter Jackson Pollock (1912–56) is famous for developing the style known as action painting. Laying a huge canvas flat on the studio floor, he poured, splashed, or dripped paint onto it. The works he produced became known as his 'drip paintings' and Pollock himself was dubbed **Jack the Dripper** (a clever variation of 'Jack the Ripper') by *Time* magazine.

❯❯ Jelly Roll

Ferdinand Joseph La Menthe Morton (1890–1941) is better known as **Jelly Roll** Morton, the US jazz pianist, composer, and band-leader. He claimed to have actually invented jazz, styling himself 'the Originator of Jazz Stomps and Blues'. In 1926 Morton formed his own band, the Red Hot Peppers, with whom he made a series of classic recordings. 'Jelly roll' is southern black slang for the sexual act or the female genitals. He may have acquired his nickname in recognition of his sexual prowess or his sideline profession of pimp. According to his own account, it came from his calling himself Sweet Papa Jelly Roll in an ad-lib when performing a vaudeville routine on stage early in his career. Among his compositions is 'Jelly Roll Blues': 'In New Orleans, Louisiana town,/ There's the finest boy for miles around/ Lord, Mister Jelly Roll, your affection he has stole.../ He's so tall and chancey,/ He's the lady's fancy./ Everyone know him,/ Certainly do adore him.'

❯❯ The Jersey Lily

Lillie Langtry (1852–1929) was a Jersey-born actress famous for her beauty and her liaison with the Prince of Wales, later Edward VII. The daughter of the Dean of Jersey, she made her stage debut in 1881, one of the first women from an aristocratic background to become an actress. Her portrait by John Millais was entitled 'A Jersey Lily' (1878).

›› Jessyenormous

The soprano Jessye Norman (b.1945) sings both opera and
concert music and has excelled in performances of works by
Wagner, Schubert, and Mahler. Her nickname
Jessyenormous, punning on her full name, rudely draws
attention to the singer's statuesque figure.

›› JFK

John Fitzgerald Kennedy (1917–63) was, at 43, the youngest
man ever to be elected US President. He grew to be seen as a
glamorous and popular world leader, particularly after the
Cuban Missile Crisis. Kennedy was assassinated while riding
in a motorcade through Dallas, Texas, in November 1963.
Like his Democratic predecessor Franklin Delano Roosevelt,
he was widely referred to by his initials. New York's main
airport is known as JFK, short for John F. Kennedy
International.

›› Jimbo

Jimmy Connors (b.1952), the US tennis player, won the
Wimbledon title in 1974 and 1982 and the US Open title five
times between 1974 and 1983. A left-hander who
popularized the two-fisted backhand, he was popularly
known as **Jimbo**.

›› Jix

The British Conservative politician William Joynson-Hicks
(1865–1932) served as Home Secretary 1924–29. His name
was originally Hicks, but he added Joynson when he married
Grace Joynson, daughter of a Manchester silk-manufacturer.
Contemporaries simply referred to him as **Jix**.

›› J.Lo

Jennifer Lopez (b.1970), the New York-born singer and film

actress of Puerto-Rican descent, is known as **J.Lo**, a name she says she was given by her fans. Her films include *Selena* (1997) and *Out of Sight* (1998) and in 2001 she released an album titled *J.Lo*. She was also once known as **La Guitarra** because her body was thought to curve like a guitar. Lopez's romance with the film actor Ben Affleck led the US press to refer to 'Hollywood's hottest couple' as **Bennifer**.

›› Joburg

The city of Johannesburg, South Africa, is informally known as **Joburg** (or **Jo'burg**), a contracted form of the name that dates from the end of the 19th century.

›› Joe Bananas

At the height of his career in the 1950s and 1960s, Mafia boss Joseph Bonanno (1905–2002) ran one of New York's five largest crime families. The press called him **Joe Bananas**, an Americanization of his name. Bonanno was involved in a Mafia power struggle in the 1960s which became known as the 'Bananas War'.

›› Johnnie

The nickname **Johnnie** (or Johnny) is traditionally attached to the surname Walker, after Johnnie Walker, a brand of whisky.

›› Jolly Jack

Jolly Jack was the writer J. B. Priestley (1894–1984), whose works include the novel *The Good Companions* (1929) and the plays *Time and the Conways* (1937) and *An Inspector Calls* (1947). During and after the Second World War he was a popular radio broadcaster on current affairs. His nickname is an ironic reference to Priestley's reputation as something of a curmudgeon.

›› Joltin' Joe

One of the most famous baseball nicknames is **Joltin' Joe**, Joe
DiMaggio (1914–99). There is a wistful reference to Joltin'
Joe in Simon and Garfunkel's song 'Mrs Robinson' (1968).
Sometimes also called the **Jolter**, DiMaggio was a player of
exceptional grace and elegance, who spent his entire career
with the New York Yankees (1936–51). In 1941 he hit in a
record-setting 56 consecutive games. He also attracted many
nicknames referring to his Italian ancestry, such as the
Wallopin' Wop, the **Roamin' Roman**, the **Little Bambino**, **Big
Giuseppe**, and **Dago**.

›› Judge

Robin Smith (b.1963), the South African-born English
cricketer, was dubbed **Judge** by his fellow players, who
thought that his hair looked like a judge's wig.

›› The Juice

The former American football player O. J. Simpson (b.1947)
was widely known in his playing days as the **Juice** or **Orange
Juice**, partly because of his ability to squeeze out of tight
places and partly from his initials. In 1995, after a long and
controversial trial which received an enormous amount of
publicity, he was acquitted of the murder of his ex-wife
Nicole Brown and her friend Ronald Goodman.

›› The Jumbo State

The **Jumbo State** is an old nickname for Texas, which has an
area of 692,405 sq km (267,338 sq miles). Until Alaska was
admitted as the 49th state of the US in 1959, Texas was the
largest state.

➤➤ K

Kenneth Clark. See ····➤ **LORD** Clark of Civilisation.

➤➤ The Kaiser

The German footballer Franz Beckenbauer (b.1945) won a record 103 international caps for West Germany (1965–77). He was the first person to win the World Cup both as team captain (in 1974) and as national coach (in 1990). Beckenbauer's nickname the **Kaiser** reflects both his commanding presence as a player and his immense influence on German football.

➤➤ Kaiser Bill

Wilhelm II (1859–1941), emperor of Germany and king of Prussia 1888–1918, was unable to prevent the outbreak of the First World War (1914), and was vilified by Allied propaganda that blamed him for the conflict. He was titled Kaiser Wilhelm (*Kaiser* being the German form of 'Caesar'), but during the war was ridiculed in Britain as **Kaiser Bill**. In 1918 he went into exile in Holland and abdicated his throne.

➤➤ Keith

Prince Philip, Duke of Edinburgh (b.1921), the husband of Elizabeth II, is lampooned as **Keith** in the satirical magazine *Private Eye*.

>> Ken Leninspart

While serving as the left-wing leader of the Greater London
Council (1981–86), Ken Livingstone (b.1945) was dubbed **Ken
Leninspart** by the satirical magazine *Private Eye*, combining
the names 'Lenin' and 'Spart'. Dave Spart was the name of the
fictional left-winger who regularly appeared in the magazine.

>> The Keystone State

The US state of Pennsylvania is the seventh or central one of
the original thirteen states, hence its nickname the **Keystone
State**. Some of the most important events in the history of
the United States took place in Pennsylvania, such as the
signing of the Declaration of Independence at Philadelphia in
1776 and the drafting of the US Constitution in the same city
in 1787.

>> The Killer

Rock-and-roller Jerry Lee Lewis (b.1935) was propelled to
fame in 1957 with the release of his single 'Whole Lotta
Shakin' Going On', which was initially banned as obscene. His
nickname **Killer** suited his 'wild man' image and ferociously
pounding piano-playing, though he acquired it in his youth.
Lewis's 1993 autobiography was inevitably titled *Killer*.

>> The King[1]

Clark Gable (1901–60) was one of the most popular male
Hollywood stars of the 1930s and 1940s. His films include *It
Happened One Night* (1934), for which he won an Oscar, and
Gone with the Wind (1939), in which he starred as Rhett
Butler. He was known as the **King of Hollywood**, or simply
the **King**, during the height of his celebrity. The title was
dismissed by the actor himself: 'This King stuff is pure bull. I
eat and drink and go to the bathroom just like anybody else.
I'm just a lucky slob from Ohio who happened to be in the
right place at the right time.'

›› The King²

Elvis Presley (1935–77) was the dominant personality of the rock-and-roll era. He shot to fame in 1956, soon becoming the most successful popular singer in the world. His many hit records include 'Heartbreak Hotel', 'Blue Suede Shoes', 'Love Me Tender', and 'Don't Be Cruel'. After making a number of films during the 1960s, he resumed his personal appearances in the 1970s, mostly in Las Vegas. He is regarded by his many admirers as the **King of Rock 'n' Roll**, or simply the **King**.

7. *Elvis Presley meets his moniker.*

›› The King³

Barry John (b.1945), the Welsh Rugby Union player, is often regarded as one of the great fly-halves in the history of the game. In 1971 he scored a record 180 points on the British Lions' tour of New Zealand.

❯❯ King Arthur

Arthur Scargill (b.1938) was leader of the National Union of
Mineworkers from 1981 to 2002. A fiery orator and combative
champion of the coal miners' cause, he led his union into the
national miners' strike 1984–85, during which the press
labelled him **King Arthur**. In 1996 Scargill broke away from
the Labour party to form the Socialist Labour Party.

❯❯ The Kingfish

Huey Long (1893–1935) was governor of Louisiana 1928–31
and state senator 1930–35. A rabble-rousing public speaker,
he is reported to have said of himself, 'For the present you
can just call me the Kingfish.' He declared his intention to run
for the presidency in 1934, but was assassinated the
following year. A kingfish is a large sea fish.

❯❯ King Kev

Kevin Keegan. See ····➤ **MIGHTY** Mouse.

❯❯ The King of Comedy

Mack Sennett (1880–1960) was the Canadian-born director
who brought the world the Keystone Kops and Charlie
Chaplin in the slapstick silent-film comedies made at his
Keystone studios (1912–35). Sennett promoted himself as
the **King of Comedy**, though he did offer this rueful comment
on the title: 'I called myself king of comedy, but I was a
harassed monarch. I worked most of the time. It was only in
the evenings that I laughed.'

❯❯ The King of Hi de Ho

The US bandleader and singer Cab Calloway (1907–94) was
known for his exuberant showmanship and striking zoot-
suited appearance. His most famous song is 'Minnie the
Moocher', which contains the refrain 'hi-de hi-de hi-de-hi,

hi-de hi-de hi-de-ho', echoed by the audience during live
performances. He made 'hi-de-ho' a national catchphrase.

›› The King of Hollywood

Clark Gable. See ····➤ The KING.

›› The King of Jazz

Swing-orchestra leader Paul Whiteman (1890–1967) did
much to make jazz widely acceptable in the US. He
promoted the first prestige jazz concert in New York in 1924,
in which he conducted the premiere of George Gershwin's
Rhapsody in Blue. From this time on, Whiteman was widely
billed as the **King of Jazz**, a promotional title he had himself
created. The label was reinforced by the Hollywood screen
biography *The King of Jazz* (1930), but has proved
controversial as the big band music he played, smoothly
orchestrated and with no improvisation, was to some purists
scarcely jazz at all.

›› The King of Pop

Michael Jackson (b.1958) was the most commercially
successful US pop star of the 1980s, with such best-selling
albums as *Thriller* (1982) and *Bad* (1987). The title the **King
of Pop** may have originally been conferred on him by his
friend Elizabeth Taylor.

›› The King of Swing

The jazz clarinettist and band-leader Benny Goodman
(1909–86) is generally credited with introducing jazz to a
mass audience. He formed his own big band in New York in
1934, and soon gained a mass following through radio and
live performances. With the arranger Fletcher Henderson, he
developed a distinctive style of big-band jazz in which an
ensemble arrangement of lively rhythm and simple melody

would incorporate the improvisations of fine soloists. He
soon became known as the **King of Swing**.

›› The King of (the) Calypso

The calypso singer Harry Belafonte (b.1927) was known as
the **King of the Calypso**, his album *Calypso* (1956), the first
to sell a million copies, spending 31 weeks at the top of the
US album chart. Belafonte's hits included 'Mary's Boy Child'
and 'Banana Boat Song' (also known as 'Day-O'). He became
a hugely successful international star, and was active in the
civil rights movement in the 1960s.

›› The King of the Cowboys

Two US film actors were known as the **King of the Cowboys**
in their day, Tom Mix and Roy Rogers. Tom Mix (1880–1940)
was a popular star of over 400 silent westerns in the 1920s
and 1930s. His films, which were action-packed and full of
stunts, included *Riders of the Purple Sage* (1925) and *King
Cowboy* (1928). Mix's character was usually dressed in white
and rode a black horse. Roy Rogers (1912–98) was a popular
singing cowboy of the 1930s and 1940s, starring mostly in
B-films. His horse was called Trigger.

›› K of K

Herbert Kitchener (1850–1916) was given the title Lord
Kitchener of Khartoum after leading the Egyptian army to
defeat the Mahdist forces at Omdurman and recapture
Khartoum in 1898. His title was often shortened to **K of K**. At
the outbreak of the First World War, as Secretary of State for
War, he was responsible for organizing the large volunteer
army which eventually fought the war on the Western Front.
His commanding image appeared on recruiting posters
urging 'Your King and Country need you'.

LI

➤➤ The Lad ('Imself)

Known as the **Lad** or the **Lad 'Imself**, the British comedian
Tony Hancock (1924–68) became a star in the 1950s with
the popular radio series *Hancock's Half Hour*, which later
successfully transferred to television (1956–61). In it he
played a lugubrious but witty misfit who is always grumbling
about suburban life. Hancock committed suicide in 1968.

➤➤ Lady Bird

Claudia Johnson (née Taylor) (b.1912) was the wife of
President Lyndon Baines Johnson. She came by her nickname
Lady Bird in childhood after her nurse Alice Tittle remarked,
'She's as pretty as a lady bird'. The name stuck, with the result
that in adult life her initials matched those of her husband.

➤➤ Lady Day

The jazz singer Billie Holiday (1915–59) began her recording
career with Benny Goodman's band in 1923, going on to
perform with numerous jazz groups. Her singing was
characterized by its dramatic intensity and highly individual
phrasing. In a notable case of mutual nicknaming, it was the
saxophonist Lester Young who first dubbed her **Lady Day**
because of her ladylike demeanour. She in turn called him
the **President**, later shortened to **Prez**. Holiday liked to be
called Lady the rest of her life. She published her
autobiography *Lady Sings the Blues* in 1956.

›› Lady Forkbender

Marcia Williams, later Lady Falkender (b.1932), was prime minister Harold Wilson's long-serving private and political secretary 1956–73. Given a life peerage in Wilson's resignation honours list in 1974, she was dubbed **Lady Forkbender** in the satirical magazine *Private Eye*. As well as playing on her name, this was a reference to the feats of Uri Geller (b.1946), the Israeli psychic performer who came to fame in the 1970s with his demonstrations of bending cutlery and stopping watches.

›› Lady Lindy

Amelia Earhart (1898–1937) was the first woman to fly the Atlantic in 1928, and the first woman to do so solo in 1932, completing the journey from Newfoundland to Londonderry in a time of 13¼ hours. Hailed as the female equivalent of Charles Lindbergh (or **Lucky Lindy**), she was dubbed **Lady Lindy**. The aircraft carrying Earhart and her navigator, Frederick J. Noonan, disappeared over the Pacific Ocean during a subsequent round-the-world flight in 1937.

›› The Laird of the Halls

The Scottish music-hall comedian Harry Lauder (1870–1950) became highly popular singing Scottish songs, many of which were his own compositions, such as 'I Love a Lassie' and 'Roamin' in the Gloamin''. He entertained troops at home and abroad in both world wars. *Laird* is the Scots form of 'lord'.

›› La Lollo

Gina Lollobrigida (b.1927) was a voluptuous Italian film star, whose Hollywood films include *Trapeze* (1956) and *Solomon and Sheba* (1959). She was often referred to as **La Lollo**.

>> The Land of Cakes

According to the poet Robert Burns, Scotland was the 'Land o' Cakes', a term referring to Scottish oatmeal cakes.

>> The Land of Enchantment

The US state of New Mexico calls itself the **Land of Enchantment**. At other times the state has promoted itself as the **Land of Heart's Desire** and the **Land of the Delight Makers**.

>> The Land of Flowers

Florida means 'flowered' in Spanish, which is why one of the US state's nicknames is the **Land of Flowers**.

>> The Land of Saints and Scholars

Ireland's nickname the **Land of Saints and Scholars** refers to the holiness and learning associated with the early Celtic Church.

>> The Land of the Free

The United States is sometimes called the **Land of the Free**. This phrase was taken from the poem by the American lawyer and verse-writer Francis Scott Key (1779–1843), which was adopted as the US national anthem in 1931: ''Tis the star-spangled banner; O long may it wave/O'er the land of the free, and the home of the brave!' ('The Star-Spangled Banner', 1814).

>> The Land of the Little Sticks

The **Land of the Little Sticks** is Canada. This comes from the Chinook word *stik* 'wood, tree, forest', the subarctic tundra region of northern Canada, characterized by its stunted vegetation.

›› The Land of the Midnight Sun

The **Land of the Midnight Sun** is a term generally applied to Lapland and the northern regions of Norway, Sweden, and Finland, where it never gets fully dark during the summer months. In the US, it is sometimes used to refer to Alaska.

›› The Land of the Rising Sun

Japan is known as the **Land of the Rising Sun**, a translation of Japanese *Nippon*, which comes from the words *nichi* 'the sun' and *pon, hon* 'source'. *Nippon* is recorded in English from the early 17th century, but *Land of the Rising Sun* is not found until the mid 19th century.

›› The Land of the Long White Cloud

The Maori name for New Zealand is Aotearoa, which literally translates as the **Land of the Long White Cloud**.

›› The Land of the Saints

The first settlers in Utah were members of the Church of Latter-Day Saints, also known as Mormons. From this comes the state's informal name the **Land of the Saints**, together with the alternative nicknames the **Land of the Mormons** and the **Mormon State**.

›› Larry Legend

The US basketball player Larry Bird (b.1956) joined the Boston Celtics in 1979, and led his team to the NBA championship in 1981, 1984, and 1986. He was voted NBA most valuable player three times (1984–86). In 1992 Bird captained the gold medal-winning US Olympic basketball team (known as the 'Dream Team'). A greatly admired forward, he was widely known as **Larry Legend**.

➤➤ The Last of the Red Hot Mommas

Sophie Tucker (1884–1966), the vaudeville and cabaret singer, was the daughter of Russian parents who emigrated to the USA. Her nickname was taken from the title of the song 'I'm the Last of the Red Hot Mommas', written by Jack Yellen, and first sung by Tucker in 1928. It fitted her brassy, dynamic image and was how she would be billed for the rest of her life. Because she was plump she was also sometimes known as **Sophie Tuckshop**.

➤➤ LBJ

As Vice-President, Lyndon Baines Johnson (1908–73) succeeded to the Presidency on J. F. Kennedy's assassination in 1963. Like his predecessor, he was known simply by his initials. Johnson ran for election in 1964 with the slogan 'All the way with LBJ'. Another slogan that came to be associated with him was 'Hey, hey, LBJ, how many kids did you kill today?', chanted by those demonstrating against US involvement in the Vietnam War.

➤➤ The Leaderene

The **Leaderene** was a humorous name for Margaret Thatcher (b.1925) while Leader of the Opposition, and later Prime Minister. Meaning 'a female leader', the word's female ending is based on forenames such as Marlene. It is thought to have been coined by the Conservative politician Norman St John Stevas.

➤➤ Lefty

Lefty is a nickname for a left-handed person. The US country singer Lefty Frizzell (1928–75) earned his nickname because as an amateur boxer he had a formidable left hook. He was born William Orville Frizzell. Lefty is also a traditional nickname in the British armed forces of any man surnamed Wright.

❯❯ The Legs

Betty Grable. See ····➤ The **GIRL** with the Million Dollar Legs.

❯❯ Lilibet

Lilibet was a childhood nickname for the future Queen
Elizabeth II, which came from her younger sister Princess
Margaret's attempt to pronounce 'Elizabeth'. It was adopted
by the rest of the royal family.

❯❯ The Lion[1]

The Italian opera singer Titta Ruffo (1877–1953) was
nicknamed the **Lion**. Noted for his rich, resonant voice, he
was also known as the **Caruso of Baritones**.

❯❯ The Lion[2]

The jazz pianist Willie Smith (1897–1973) was a flamboyant
showman, a braggart, and sharp dresser. His nickname was
probably given to him by fellow-pianist James P. Johnson,
though exactly why he called Smith the **Lion** isn't certain. It
may derive from his bravery at the front in the First World
War or from his devotion to Judaism which led to him being
called 'the Lion of Judah'. Smith would announce his arrival
in a club with the words 'The Lion is here!' He is the subject
of Duke Ellington's composition 'Portrait of The Lion' (1940).

❯❯ The Lion of Judah

Born Ras Tafari Makonnen, Haile Selassie (1892–1975) was
emperor of Ethiopia 1930–74. As a statesman he is credited
with modernizing his country and making it a prominent
force in Africa. He is held in reverence as the Messiah by the
Rastafarian religious movement, which is named after him.
Haile Selassie was known as the **Lion of Judah**, one of the
titles of the emperor of Ethiopia, deriving from the reference

to Christ in the Book of Revelation as 'the Lion of the tribe of Judah'. The emblem of the Lion of Judah, symbolizing strength, used to appear on the Ethiopian national flag: a crowned lion carrying a flagstaff flying the national colours of red, gold, and green.

❯❯ The Lion of Vienna

The footballer Nat Lofthouse (b.1925) played for Bolton Wanderers and England. He was dubbed the **Lion of Vienna** following his barnstorming performance during England's 3–2 win over Austria in 1952. The *Lion of Vienna* pub in Bolton, named after him, was opened by the player himself in 1984.

❯❯ The Lions

Millwall football club was founded in 1885 by workers at the J. T. Morton jam and marmalade factory in West Ferry Road, on the Isle of Dogs, London. Since many of the early players were Scots, the club adopted the Scottish flag's lion rampant for its badge and was soon known by its supporters as the **Lions**. Since 1910 the club's ground has been appropriately named The Den.

❯❯ Little America

Grosvenor Square, London has had links with the United States since John Adams, the first minister to Britain (1785–88) and later President, occupied No. 9. The US Embassy stands on the west side and in the centre of the square is a bronze statue of President Franklin D. Roosevelt. No. 20 was General Eisenhower's headquarters during the Second World War, when the square became popularly known as **Little America**.

❯❯ Little Cuba

Miami, Florida is known as **Little Cuba** because of its large Cuban immigrant population.

❯❯ The Little Flower

As mayor of New York City 1933–45, Fiorello La Guardia
(1882–1947) tackled the city's poverty and housing
problems and fought corruption and organized crime. He
was known as the **Little Flower**, a translation of his Italian
first name. New York's La Guardia airport, the construction
of which he successfully campaigned for, is named after
him.

❯❯ The Little Master

Donald Bradman. See ····➤ The **DON**.

❯❯ Little Miss Poker Face

Helen Wills Moody (1905–98) dominated women's tennis
in the 1920s and 1930s. She was Wimbledon champion eight
times and US champion seven times, winning 31 grand slam
titles in all. Journalists dubbed her **Little Miss Poker Face**
because her expression on court never gave any indication
of her feelings. She was also known as the **Queen of the
Courts**.

❯❯ Little Mo

Tennis player Maureen Connolly (1934–69) won the US
singles title aged 16, losing only four matches throughout the
rest of her career. In 1953 Connolly became the first woman
to win the grand slam by taking all four major titles (British,
US, French, and Australian). Her career was ended by injury
when she was 19. Only 5ft 2ins (157cm) tall, she was
affectionately known as **Little Mo**.

❯❯ Little Rhody

The US state of Rhode Island, the smallest state in the Union,
is popularly known as **Little Rhody**.

❯❯ Little Sparrow

Edith Piaf (1915–63) started her career as a street singer at the age of 15 and went on to become the best-loved singer in France, mourned by the whole country at her death. She is remembered for the poignancy and passion with which she sang such songs as 'La vie en rose' and 'Je ne regrette rien'. Piaf was born Edith Giovanna Gassion and both her stage name and her nickname come from the cabaret impresario Louis Leplee in 1935 calling her *la mome piaf* (meaning 'little sparrow') because of her small size.

❯❯ Little Venice

Little Venice is an area of London at the west end of Regent's Canal, a secluded and attractive canal basin noted for its artists. Both Robert Browning and Lord Byron compared the area to Venice, but the name **Little Venice** was not in general usage until after the Second World War.

❯❯ The Livermore Larruper

The boxer Max Baer (1909–59) was born in Omaha, Nebraska, but he was brought up in Livermore, California. Baer was billed as the **Livermore Larruper** ('larrup' meaning to beat or thrash someone) when he turned professional in 1929. He became world heavyweight champion in 1934, defeating Primo Carnera.

❯❯ The Lizard King

Jim Morrison (1943–71) was the flamboyant lead singer with the Doors, a rock group associated with the drug culture, avant-garde art, and psychedelia of the late 1960s. Their songs, broodingly performed by Morrison, included 'Light My Fire' (1967) and 'Riders on the Storm' (1971). He referred to himself as the **Lizard King**, a title first used in his poem 'The Celebration of the Lizard King', printed on the sleeve of the album *Waiting for the Sun* (1968).

›› The Lizard of Oz

In 1995, on a state visit by the Queen to his country, the Australian prime minister Paul Keating (b.1944) put his arm around the Queen, a severe breach of royal protocol. A vociferous republican, Keating was vilified in the British press as the **Lizard of Oz**, echoing the title of the children's book and film *The Wizard of Oz*.

›› Lone Eagle

The **Lone Eagle** was Charles Lindbergh (1902–74), the US aviator who made the first nonstop solo transatlantic flight in 1927. Lindbergh's baby son Charles was popularly known as the **Little Eaglet**.

›› The Lone Star State

The 'lone star' is the single star on the state flag of Texas, hence the state's well-known nickname, the **Lone Star State**. A single star was also depicted on the flag of the Texas Republic (1836–45).

›› The Long Fellow[1]

Eamon de Valera (1882–1975) served as Taoiseach (Irish Prime Minister) 1937–48, 1951–4, and 1957–9 and President of the Republic of Ireland 1959–73. Tall and lean, de Valera was affectionately nicknamed the **Long Fellow**, in contrast to Michael Collins, the **Big Fellow**.

›› The Long Fellow[2]

The English jockey Lester Piggott (b.1935) rode 30 Classic winners and won the Derby a record nine times. He was the champion jockey nine times between 1960 and 1971 and again in 1981 and 1982. Tall (5ft 9ins) for a jockey, he was known as the **Long Fellow**.

>> Lord Clark of Civilisation

Kenneth Clark (1903–83) was a British art historian and
Director of the National Gallery 1934–45. His television
series *Civilisation*, first broadcast in 1969, popularized the
history of art. When he was made a life peer in 1969, he took
the title Lord Clark of Saltwood, though the satirical
magazine *Private Eye* referred to him as **Lord Clark of
Civilisation**. He was also known simply as **K**.

>> Lord Haw-Haw

During the Second World War, William Joyce (1906–46),
born in the US of Irish parentage, made propaganda
broadcasts in English from Nazi Germany. The nickname
Lord Haw-Haw was coined by the *Daily Express* journalist
Jonah Barrington, referring to Joyce's drawling nasal
delivery, with which he affected an upper-class accent. He
was hanged for treason after the war.

>> Lord Porn

In the early 1970s the Earl of Longford, Frank Pakenham
(1905–2001) became known in the press as **Lord Porn**
because of his zealous campaigning against pornography and
sexual liberation. In 1972 he headed an unofficial inquiry
into pornography in the UK. Lord Longford was also known
as a campaigner for prison reform.

>> The Louisville Lip

Muhammad Ali (b.1942) was the first boxer to be world
heavyweight champion three times. He was born Cassius
Marcellus Clay (by which name he was known until changing
it to Muhammad Ali in 1964) in Louisville, Kentucky. Early
on in his career he was known as a brash, bantering
loudmouth. He recited doggerel verse in which he would
predict the round he would knock out his opponent and told

everyone he was 'the Greatest'. The press had a field day
coining colourful nicknames for him such as **Gaseous Cassius**,
Cash the Brash, and the **Mouth**, but the name which really
caught on was the **Louisville Lip**. In 1964, Cassius Clay (as he
then still was) entered the ring for his first world
heavyweight title fight against Sonny Liston with 'The Lip'
stitched on the back of his white robe.

▶▶ The Love Goddess

Rita Hayworth (1918–87), red-headed and voluptuous, was
one of the most glamorous film stars of the 1940s. She was
the vivacious star of a succession of film musicals including
Cover Girl (1944) and also played leading roles in several
films of the film noir genre, notably *Gilda* (1946) and *The
Lady from Shanghai* (1948). Hayworth was dubbed
Hollywood's **Love Goddess** at the height of her career.

▶▶ The Lucky Country

In his book *The Lucky Country*, published in 1964, Donald
Horne (b.1921) argued that Australia had become a
complacent, inward-looking country. The term is often used
ironically to refer to Australia as a land of opportunity.

▶▶ Lucky Lindy

In May 1927, Charles Lindbergh (1902–74) made the first
nonstop solo transatlantic flight in his single-engined
monoplane *Spirit of St Louis*, taking 33½ hours from New
York to Paris. He became a national celebrity on his return
home and was awarded the Congressional Medal of Honor.
His two-year-old son was kidnapped and murdered in 1932,
after which Lindbergh moved to Europe.

▶▶ Lucky Lucan

The Earl of Lucan, Richard John Bingham (b.1934), known
as **Lucky Lucan** because of his success at gambling, was a

British peer who mysteriously disappeared in November 1974
on the night that his wife was attacked and his children's
nanny was murdered. Lord Lucan has never been found, and
speculation about his survival and whereabouts continues to
this day.

>> Lucky Luciano

Charles Luciano (born Salvatore Luciana) (1896–1962)
became known as the gangster **Lucky** Luciano. His nickname
stemmed from an incident in which he survived having his
throat slit by a rival gangster.

▶▶ Macca

Macca is a common nickname for someone from Liverpool who's name begins Mc or Mac. The two most famous Liverpudlian Maccas are Paul McCartney (b.1942) and Steve McManaman (b.1972). McCartney was a founder member of the Beatles and wrote most of their songs in collaboration with John Lennon. McManaman is an English footballer who has played for Liverpool, Real Madrid, and Manchester City.

▶▶ Machine Gun Kelly

The US bankrobber and kidnapper George R. Kelly (born George Kelly Barnes) (1895–1954) was given his underworld nickname **Machine Gun Kelly** by his wife. He married Kathryn Thorne in 1927 and it is she who is said to have bought Kelly his first machine gun. She encouraged him to practise shooting walnuts off fence posts.

▶▶ Mac the Knife[1]

Harold Macmillan (1894–1986) was British Prime Minister 1957–63. He received the nickname **Mac the Knife** after sacking seven cabinet ministers in 1962 in what became known as the Night of the Long Knives. The nickname is a deliberate echo of Mack the Knife, the murderous character from Brecht and Weill's *The Threepenny Opera* (1929), himself based on Macheath the highwayman in John Gay's *The Beggar's Opera* (1728).

❯❯ Mac the Knife[2]

Ian MacGregor (b.1912) was chairman of British Steel
(1980–83) and the British Coal Board (1983–86).
MacGregor was originally dubbed **Mac the Knife** by the trade
unions because of the drastic staff cuts he implemented in
the steel industry in order to make it profitable. Later, the
nickname was widely used during the British miners' strike of
1984–85.

❯❯ Mac the Mouth

John McEnroe. See ····❯ SUPERBRAT.

❯❯ Madchester

In the late 1980s and early 1990s, the city of Manchester was
dubbed **Madchester** in the press in reference to its place at
the centre of the UK rock music scene, dominated by such
bands as the Happy Mondays, the Stone Roses, and Inspiral
Carpets.

❯❯ Madge

The pop singer Madonna (born Madonna Louise Ciccone)
(b.1958) rose to international stardom in the mid-1980s
through her records and accompanying videos, cultivating
her image as a sex symbol and frequently courting
controversy. Following her marriage to the British film
director Guy Ritchie, the British press dubbed her **Madge**, in
a jokey attempt to cast her as a suburban housewife. The
singer has expressed her dislike of the nickname; in January
2002 a front-page story in the *Daily Star* was headlined
'Don't Call Me Madge'.

❯❯ The Mad Monk

The British Conservative politician Keith Joseph (1918–94)
was a close political adviser to Margaret Thatcher, generally

credited with being the intellectual architect of her free-market ideology. His nickname the **Mad Monk** derived from his austere, intense demeanour and his reputation for agonizing over an issue. It was originally coined by his fellow Conservative Chris Patten. The original **Mad Monk** was the Russian monk Grigori Rasputin (1871–1916), notorious for exercising great influence over Tsar Nicholas II and his family. Rasputin's abuse of power, combined with his reputation for debauchery, led him to be eventually assassinated by a group of noblemen loyal to the tsar.

▶▶ Maggie

Maggie was the most common nickname for Margaret Thatcher (b.1925) used in the British popular press, especially in headlines, during the time she was prime minister.

▶▶ Magic

Basketball player Earvin Johnson (b.1959) is universally known as **Magic** Johnson. He was first called Magic as a 15-year-old at high school, a nickname coined by Michigan sports writer Fred Stabley Jr who had seen him play. Johnson, known for his dazzling passing and ball-handling, won five NBA championships with the Los Angeles Lakers.

▶▶ The Magnificent Wildcat

Pola Negri (1897–1987) was a Polish-born US film actress who starred in silent Hollywood films of the 1920s. Negri, billed as the **Magnificent Wildcat**, was a tempestuous and flamboyant actress who specialized in playing exotic vamps. Her real-life lovers included Charlie Chaplin and Rudolph Valentino.

▶▶ The Magnolia State

The emblem of the US state of Mississippi is the magnolia flower, hence the state's nickname the **Magnolia State**.

›› The Magpies

Newcastle United football club are known as the **Magpies**
because of the black-and-white stripes the team play in. Notts
County football club are similarly nicknamed for the same
reason.

›› The Mailman

Admirers of US basketball player Karl Malone (b.1963) call
him the **Mailman** because he 'always delivers'. The nickname
was coined by a local sportswriter when Malone was
playing college basketball at Louisiana Tech. He played his
first 18 NBA seasons with the Utah Jazz, joining the Los
Angeles Lakers in 2003. Malone is the second leading career
scorer in NBA league history, ranking behind only Kareem
Abdul-Jabbar.

›› The Manassa Mauler

Jack Dempsey (1895–1983) was world heavyweight
champion 1919–26, during which time he drew extremely
large audiences to boxing. His defence of the title in 1921
(against Georges Carpentier) was the first fight at which a
million dollars was taken at the gate. Born in Manassa,
Colorado, William Harrison Dempsey adopted the name Jack
after 'Nonpareil' Jack Dempsey, a famous middleweight
champion from the end of the 19th century. Sports writers
dubbed him the **Manassa Mauler** because of the ferocity and
aggression he displayed in the ring.

›› Mandy

Peter Mandelson (b.1953) is often regarded as one of the
architects of the Labour Party's victory in the 1997 general
election. He twice held cabinet posts, but was forced to
resign each of them in controversial circumstances, first in
1998 and a second time in 2001. He is informally known as
Mandy, an abbreviation of his surname and perhaps

originally a subtle allusion to his sexuality before it was publicly revealed that he was gay.

◆◆ The Man from Missouri

Harry S. Truman (1884–1972) was president of the US 1945–53. Raised on a farm near Independence, Missouri, Truman was sometimes known as the **Man from Missouri**.

◆◆ The Man in Black

Johnny Cash (1932–2003) was a US country music singer and songwriter who, in a career spanning six decades, had such hits as 'I Walk the Line' (1956), 'Ring of Fire' (1963), and 'A Boy Named Sue' (1969). He was known for his gruff baritone voice and for always wearing black on stage. This dated back to his debut at the Grand Ole Opry in 1957, a contrast to the sequins and rhinestones worn by other country singers. Cash later began to be billed as the **Man in Black**, following a 1971 hit of that title.

◆◆ The Man of a Thousand Faces

The US film actor Lon Chaney (1883–1930) usually played deformed or monstrous characters in more than 150 silent films, including *The Hunchback of Notre Dame* (1923) and *The Phantom of the Opera* (1925). He was a master of make-up and became known as the **Man of a Thousand Faces**. This was also the title of the 1957 film biography of the actor, starring James Cagney.

◆◆ The Man on the Wedding Cake

Republican Thomas E. Dewey (1902–71) unsuccessfully ran for US president in 1944 and 1948. The disparaging nickname the **Man on the Wedding Cake** (or the **Bridegroom on the Wedding Cake**), originally coined by Grace Hodgson Flandrau in 1948, drew attention to Dewey's short stature, his black moustache, and his total lack of charisma. It delighted Alice Roosevelt Longworth (1884–1980), daughter of Theodore Roosevelt, who widely repeated the jibe and it is often attributed to her.

▶▶ The Man with the Orchid-lined Voice

Enrico Caruso (1873–1921) is usually considered the greatest operatic tenor of the 20th century. His greatest successes were in operas by Verdi, Puccini, and Jules Massenet. Caruso was the first major tenor to be recorded on gramophone records; it was said that 'Caruso made the gramophone, and the gramophone made Caruso'. The baritone-like warmth and velvety smoothness of his voice earned him the title the **Man with the Orchid-lined Voice**, coined by his PR man Edward Bernays.

▶▶ The Man You Love To Hate

The Austrian-born US actor and director Erich von Stroheim (1885–1957) usually played villainous roles, notably in the 1918 propaganda film *The Heart of Humanity*, in which he was first billed as the **Man You Love to Hate**. He went on to play a succession of sadistic Prussian or German officers in such films as *La Grande Illusion* (1937).

▶▶ The March King

John Philip Sousa (1854–1932), the US composer and conductor, wrote more than 100 marches, such as 'Liberty Bell', 'The Stars and Stripes Forever', 'King Cotton', and 'Hands Across the Sea'. The sousaphone, invented in 1898, was named in his honour.

▶▶ Marks and Sparks

Marks and Spencer, a British chain of clothes and food stores, was originally founded as the Marks and Spencer Penny Bazaars by Michael Marks (1863–1907) and Thomas Spencer (*c.*1852–1904). The informal and humorous name **Marks and Sparks** dates from the 1940s.

❯❯ Marvelous Marvin

Shaven-skulled Marvin Hagler (b.1952) was world
middleweight champion 1980–87. In 1982 the boxer had his
name legally changed by deed poll to **Marvelous Marvin
Hagler**.

❯❯ The Ma State

New South Wales was the earliest Australian colony to be
founded, hence its nickname the **Ma State**.

❯❯ The Master[1]

To his many admirers the writer W. Somerset Maugham
(1874–1965) was the **Master**. His novels include *Of Human
Bondage* (1915), *The Moon and Sixpence* (1919), and *Cakes
and Ale* (1930). Maugham was an expert writer of short
stories, some of which are considered among the best ever
written in English.

❯❯ The Master[2]

The US film director D. W. Griffith (1875–1948) was a
pioneer in the development of cinema. Known in Hollywood
as the **Master**, he introduced the techniques of close-ups,
cross-cutting, fade-out, moving-camera shots, and flashback
in such films as his epic of the American Civil War *The Birth
of a Nation* (1915) and *Intolerance* (1916).

❯❯ The Master[3]

Jack Hobbs (1882–1963) is often regarded as the finest
English batsman of the 20th century, hence his nickname the
Master. In a cricket career that lasted nearly 30 years, Hobbs
scored 61,237 first-class runs and 197 centuries (1905–34).
He first played for England in 1907 and went on to play in 61
Tests.

❯❯ The Master[4]

Noël Coward (1899–1973) disliked the title the **Master**, which had also been applied to the writer Somerset Maugham (1874–1965) and the US film director D. W. Griffith (1875–1948). His own comment on the label was 'Oh, you know, jack of all trades, master of none...'. Coward was certainly prolific. As well as plays such as *Hay Fever* (1925) and *Private Lives* (1930), he wrote revues and musicals, including *Cavalcade* (1931). Among his many songs is 'Mad Dogs and Englishmen' (1932). Coward's films (as writer and producer) include *In Which We Serve* (1942) and *Brief Encounter* (1945).

❯❯ The Master of Suspense

Alfred Hitchcock. See ····➤ HITCH.

❯❯ The Match King

After he founded the United Swedish Match Company in 1913, Ivar Kreuger (1880–1932) set out to control the worldwide match industry in the 1920s through a series of acquisitions. Known as the **Match King**, the Swedish industrialist and financier eventually controlled three-quarters of the world's production of matches. His empire collapsed with the Great Depression and, following the disclosure that it had been built on forgery and fraudulent deals, he committed suicide in 1932.

❯❯ Maximum John

The US federal judge John J. Sirica (1904–92) became famous during his participation in the Watergate prosecutions of the 1970s. His nickname **Maximum John** was due to his uncompromising reputation for stiff sentences. Sirica's rulings were reversed on appeal more often than those of most judges.

8. *The Mekon*

›› The Mekon

The British politician William Hague (b.1961) was leader of
the Conservative Party 1997–2001. During his tenure as the
leader of the Opposition, Hague attracted the
uncomplimentary nickname the **Mekon**, referring to his bald
head. The Mekon is Dan Dare's arch-enemy in the comic strip
by Frank Hampson which appeared in the *Eagle* comic
between 1950 and 1967. He originates from the planet
Venus, is green-skinned, and has a small body and an
enormous bald head.

›› The Merry Millers

Rotherham football club's ground is called Millmoor, from
whose name the club get their nickname the **Merry Millers**.

›› The Mersey Funnel

The Roman Catholic Cathedral (Christ the King) in Liverpool
is known locally as the **Mersey Funnel**. The nickname comes
from the distinctive shape of the cathedral's central lantern
tower and puns on the Mersey Tunnel that provides a link
under the River Mersey between Liverpool and Birkenhead.
The cathedral is also known as ····▶ **PADDY'S** Wigwam.

❯❯ The Met

Two institutions are familiarly known as the **Met**; in each case this is an abbreviation of the word *Metropolitan*. In Britain, the term is used for the Metropolitan Police in London. In the US, it is used for the Metropolitan Opera House (and Company) in New York.

❯❯ The Microwave

Basketball player Vinnie Johnson (b.1956) played guard for the Detroit Pistons in the 1980s and early 90s. He was nicknamed the **Microwave**, originally by Boston Celtic's Danny Ainge, because he could come off the bench and heat up in seconds, starting to score immediately. A shot of Johnson's famously won the 1990 NBA championship with seven-tenths of a second left on the clock.

❯❯ Mighty Mouse

Kevin Keegan (b.1951) was a star striker for Liverpool in the 1970s, for whom he made 230 league appearances, and played for England 63 times. His managerial career at club level has included periods at Newcastle United, Fulham, and Manchester City, and he has also managed the England team (1999–2000). Relatively small in stature, Keegan became known as **Mighty Mouse**, after the well-known cartoon character, while playing in Germany for SV Hamburg. His later managerial exploits at Newcastle led to him being crowned **King Kev** by the fans.

❯❯ The Mile High City

Denver, Colorado, is situated at an altitude of 1,608m (5,280 ft) near the foothills of the Rocky Mountains, hence its nickname the **Mile High City**.

›› The Milk Snatcher

As Minister of Education in Edward Heath's government (1970–74), Margaret Thatcher (b.1925) abolished free school milk for children over the age of eight, earning herself the rhyming nickname Thatcher the **Milk Snatcher**.

›› Ming

Robert Menzies (1894–1978) was Australia's longest-serving prime minister (1939–41 and 1949–66), presiding over a period of economic prosperity for his country. Known for his autocratic style of leadership, he was nicknamed **Ming** after Ming the Merciless, the evil emperor who appeared in the Flash Gordon comic strip. There is also a nod to the Scottish pronunciation of his surname, 'Ming-ies'. Menzies' long second term became known as the 'Ming Dynasty', after the Chinese dynasty founded in 1368 by Zhu Yuanzhang.

›› Miss Frigidaire

US tennis player Chris Evert (b.1954) won both the US and French Open championships six times and three Wimbledon titles (1974, 1976, 1981). Evert was dubbed **Miss Frigidaire** by the British press because of her cool, unruffled manner on court.

›› The Modfather

Paul Weller (b.1958) is a British singer and songwriter whose albums include *Wild Wood* (1994) and *Stanley Road* (1995). He has been labelled the **Modfather**, a reference to the part he played in the 1970s mod revival with his group the Jam and to his influence on a younger generation of musicians in bands such as Oasis and Ocean Colour Scene. The nickname is a combination of the words *mod* and *godfather*.

›› Mogadon Man

Geoffrey Howe (b.1926) served as Chancellor of the
Exchequer 1979–83, Foreign Secretary 1983–89, and
deputy prime minister 1984–90. Parliamentary
correspondents called him **Mogadon Man** because of the
supposedly sleep-inducing effect of his speeches. Mogadon is
the proprietary name for a tranquillizing drug used to treat
insomnia.

›› The Monkey State

In the US, the **Monkey State** is Tennessee. This mocking
nickname harks back to the famous Monkey Trial of 1925, in
which schoolteacher Thomas Scopes was found guilty of
teaching the Darwinian theory of evolution, at that time
prohibited in any Tennessee schools supported by public
funds.

›› Monty

In 1942 Field Marshal Bernard Montgomery (1887–1976)
commanded the 8th Army in the Western Desert, where his
victory at El Alamein proved the first significant Allied
success in the Second World War. He was later given
command of the Allied ground forces in the invasion of
Normandy in 1944 and received the German surrender in
1945. He was affectionately known as **Monty**. Among
various derivations that have been proposed for the
expression 'the full monty' (meaning the full amount
possible, the works) is Montgomery's apparent insistence on
eating a full English breakfast.

›› The Monumental City

The US city of Baltimore in Maryland is nicknamed the
Monumental City (or the **Monument City**) on account of the
Washington Monument, the first erected to George
Washington, and its other monuments.

❯❯ Mormon City

Salt Lake City, founded by Brigham Young, is the world headquarters of the Church of Latter-Day Saints, also known as Mormons.

❯❯ The Mosquito State

In the 1880s and 90s New Jersey was known as the **Mosquito State** because of the swarms of insects from the New Jersey marshes that plagued New York City at that time.

❯❯ Moss Bros

Moss Bros, pronounced 'Moss Bross', is the informal name for Moss Brothers, a British firm of tailors and outfitters associated with the hire of formal clothes.

❯❯ The Mother of Presidents

The US state of Virginia was the birthplace of eight US presidents, including four of the first five: Washington, Jefferson, Madison, and Monroe. The title the **Mother of Presidents** has also been claimed by the state of Ohio, birthplace of seven presidents including Grant, Garfield, and Taft.

❯❯ The Mother of States

There are two reasons why Virginia is appropriately nicknamed the **Mother of States**. Firstly, the first permanent English settlement in North America was founded at Jamestown, Virginia in 1607. More significantly, all or part of eight other states (namely, Illinois, Indiana, Kentucky, Michigan, Minnesota, Ohio, West Virginia, and Wisconsin) were formed from western territory originally claimed by Virginia.

▶▶ The Mother of the Blues

Ma Rainey (1886–1939), the US blues singer, is said to have taught Bessie Smith, though she only began making records herself a year after Smith did. Her recording career (mostly 1923–29) was short but prolific. Born Gertrude Malissa Nix Pridgett, she disliked the title Ma Rainey (which she acquired after marrying William 'Pa' Rainey in 1904, with whom she formed a song and dance team), preferring to be addressed as Madame Rainey.

▶▶ Motor City

Detroit. See ····▶ **MOTOWN**.

▶▶ Motown

The city of Detroit, Michigan, is the centre of the US automobile industry. Its nickname **Motown** is an abbreviation of 'Motor Town'. The record company Tamla Motown was founded by Barry Gordy in Detroit in 1959. Detroit is also known as **Motor City**.

▶▶ The Mountain State

The US state of West Virginia is known as the **Mountain State**. Almost 80% of the state lies in the rugged and mountainous Allegheny Plateau.

▶▶ The Mouth

Muhammad Ali. See ····▶ The **LOUISVILLE** Lip.

▶▶ Mr Five-Per-Cent

Mr Five-Per-Cent was Calouste Gulbenkian (1869–1955), the Turkish-born British oil magnate and philanthropist of Armenian descent who founded the Gulbenkian Foundation, to which he left his large fortune and art collection. His nickname stemmed from his retaining a 5% interest in the Iraq Petroleum Co., a company he founded.

›› Mr October

The US baseball player Reggie Jackson (b.1946) was dubbed **Mr October** because of his heroic performances in the World Series, which takes place in October after the end of the season. In the 1977 World Series he hit three home runs in one game.

›› Mr Saturday Night

In the 1950s Jackie Gleason (1916–87) was an ever-present fixture on Saturday night television in the US, first hosting the variety show *Cavalcade of Stars* and then starring in the popular television series *The Honeymooners*. The portly comedian thus came to be known as **Mr Saturday Night**.

›› Mr Teasie Weasie

Raymond (born Raymond Pierre Carlo Bessone) (1911–92) was a London hairdresser who, in the early 1950s, regularly demonstrated hairdressing on a television show called *Quite Contrary*. His nickname **Mr Teasie Weasie** was a reference to his catchphrase 'A teasie-weasie here, and a teasie-weasie there'.

›› Mr Television

Milton Berle (1908–2002) was an enormous star of US television in the 1950s. Having worked in vaudeville, he made his debut in television in 1948, as the host of the variety show *Texaco Star Theater* (later *The Milton Berle Show*). The show, which helped to establish television as a popular medium, was characterized by irreverent humour, slapstick, dreadful puns, and general buffoonery. Berle became affectionately known to his audiences as **Mr Television** and **Uncle Miltie**.

›› Muddy

The nickname **Muddy** is traditionally prefixed to the surname Waters, after the blues musician Muddy Waters (1915–83). Born McKinley Morganfield, he was given the nickname Muddy (later lengthened to Muddy Waters) because as a boy he liked playing near a muddy creek in Clarksdale, Mississippi.

›› Muscles

Australian tennis player Ken Rosewall (b.1934) won 18 Grand Slam titles, including the Australian four times (1953, 1955, 1971–72), the French twice (1953, 1968), and the US twice (1956, 1970). He failed to win the Wimbledon singles title, although he played in three finals. As a teenager he was given the ironic nickname **Muscles** because he looked so skinny.

›› The Muscles from Brussels

Jean-Claude Van Damme (b.1961) rejoices in the nickname the **Muscles from Brussels**. The Belgian film actor and former kickboxing champion has starred in such action films as *Double Impact* (1991), *Universal Soldier* (1992), and *Hard Target* (1993).

The Nabob of Sob

Johnnie Ray. See ····▶ The PRINCE of Wails.

Nasty

The Romanian tennis player Ilie Nastase (b.1946) won the US Open in 1972 and the French Open in 1973. A flamboyant and controversial player, he was known as **Nasty**, punning on his surname, because of his volatile temper and gamesmanship on court.

The Navel of the Nation

Kansas lies in the geographical centre of the United States (or, strictly speaking the 48 contiguous states), hence its nickname the **Navel of the Nation**.

Neddy

The National Economic Development Council was formed in 1962 as a forum for economic consultation between government, management, and trade unions, in order to plan ways of increasing growth and efficiency in British industry. Known informally as **Neddy** from its initials, the NEDC also set up other committees to study conditions in individual industries. These were accordingly dubbed **Little Neddies**.

>> The News of the Screws

The News of the World is a popular British Sunday newspaper with a reputation for publishing lurid stories about the sex lives of celebrities, hence its nickname the **News of the Screws**.

>> Night Train

The American footballer Dick Lane (1928–2002) played cornerback for the Los Angeles Rams, the Chicago Cardinals, and the Detroit Lions. Early in his career, at a Los Angeles Rams training camp, the rookie Lane used to spend hours talking to the veteran player Tom Fears, who always seemed to be playing the Buddy Morrow jazz record *Night Train*. This became Lane's nickname. A ferocious tackler, Lane was famous for wrapping his arms round an opposing player's throat and bringing him down to the ground. This manoeuvre, known as the 'Night Train Necktie', was eventually outlawed by the NFL.

>> Nobby

Nobby is a common nickname for someone with the surname Clark or Clarke. *Nobby* means very smart or elegant, from *nob*, an upper-class person, a member of the nobility. Clerks working in the City were once regarded as *nobby* because they used to be smartly dressed in top hats.

>> The North Star State

At one time Minnesota was the northernmost state in the Union, and it still retains the motto *'L'Étoile du Nord'* ('The North Star') on the state seal and flag. This explains its official nickname the **North Star State**.

>> Nosey Parker

As Archbishop of Canterbury during the early part of Elizabeth I's reign (1559–75), Matthew Parker (1504–75) guided the Church of England on a moderate course between Roman Catholicism and extreme Protestantism. He is associated with the nickname **Nosey Parker**, said to refer to his reputation for being overinquisitive about ecclesiastical matters. The term has come to be applied to any prying person or a busybody. **Nosey** is traditionally a common nickname for anyone with the surname Parker, especially in the armed forces.

» The Nutmeg State

Connecticut's nickname the **Nutmeg State** comes from the popular tradition that the early settlers of the state were so crafty that they could sell nutmeg-shaped pieces of wood to the gullible. Hence, in the US, a 'wooden nutmeg' is a false or fraudulent thing.

⟫ The Ocean State

Bordered by the Atlantic Ocean, Rhode Island in the US promotes itself to tourists as the **Ocean State**.

⟫ Ol' Blue Eyes

Although he had announced his retirement two years previously, Frank Sinatra (1915–98) marked his comeback in 1973 with the album *Ol' Blue Eyes is Back*. The following year he was back performing on stage. The tag is said to have been coined by publicity man Lee Solters.

⟫ Old Big 'Ead

As a football manager Brian Clough (b.1935) won the League championship in 1972 with Derby County and the European Cup in 1979 and 1980 with Nottingham Forest. Famously outspoken and opinionated, he was known as **Old Big 'Ead** or **Cloughie**. The former nickname was coined by his wife when he was awarded the OBE for services to football: she said that was what the letters stood for.

⟫ The Old Colony

The **Old Colony** is the US state of Massachusetts. This refers to the original Plymouth Colony founded by the Pilgrim Fathers in Massachusetts in 1620. Another settlement, the Massachusetts Bay Colony, was founded in Salem in 1628.

❯❯ The Old Dart

In Australia and New Zealand, the **Old Dart** is an informal name for England, with *Dart* representing a dialect pronunciation of *dirt*.

❯❯ The Old Dominion

In 1660 Virginia was the first British possession in America to accept the restored monarch Charles II as its king. He subsequently accorded the colony the status of a dominion, hence its long-standing nickname the **Old Dominion**.

❯❯ The Old Groaner

Bing Crosby (1904–77) was affectionately known as the **Old Groaner**, a reference to his soft, husky baritone and the relaxed style of singing (known as crooning) he popularized. His songs include 'Pennies from Heaven' and 'White Christmas', the latter of which has sold over 30 million copies.

❯❯ Old Hopalong

During his presidency, Ronald Reagan (1911–2004) was caricatured in Britain as **Old Hopalong**, a nickname coined by

9. Old Hopalong

the satirical magazine *Private Eye*. In his former career as a movie actor, Reagan had often played cowboys in westerns. Hopalong Cassidy was a fictional cowboy who had a limp and was dressed in black. He was created by the writer Clarence E. Mulford and played in films and a television series by the US actor William Boyd.

➤➤ The Old Lady of Threadneedle Street

The Bank of England stands in London's Threadneedle Street. The bank's famous nickname dates from the late 18th century, as a caption to James Gillray's cartoon of 22 May 1797, 'Political Ravishment, or The Old Lady of Threadneedle-Street in danger!' showing the 'Old Lady' dressed in one-pound notes, seated on a strong-box containing her gold, with Pitt placing an arm round her waist and a hand in her pocket. He has dropped a scroll of forced 'loans'. The Old Lady is screaming, 'Murder! Murder! Rape! Murder!...Ruin, Ruin, Ruin!' In the pediment of the facade's portico there now stands a statue of the Old Lady of Threadneedle Street holding a model of the building on her knee.

➤➤ The Old Line State

In American colonial times, the state of Maryland was the dividing line between the Crown land grants of Lord Baltimore and those of William Penn, hence its nickname the **Old Line State**.

➤➤ The Old North State

The US state of North Carolina is sometimes called the **Old North State**, because of its geographical position and history. Sir Walter Raleigh tried unsuccessfully to establish a colony on Roanoke Island in the 1580s. The first permanent settlement was in 1663.

›› Old Slowhand

London graffiti in the mid-60s used to proclaim 'Clapton is God'. A virtuoso of the electric guitar with a seemingly effortless technique, Eric Clapton (b.1945) played in the Yardbirds (1963–65) and then formed his own group, Cream (1966–68). He later developed a more restrained style, reflected in his nickname **Slowhand**, also the title of one of his albums (1977).

›› Old Squiffy

Herbert Henry Asquith. See ····➤ SQUIFFY.

›› Old Stoneface

Buster Keaton (1895–1966), noted for his deadpan expression, acrobatic skills, and elaborate stunts, was one of the biggest stars of silent comedy. Films he directed and starred in include *Sherlock Junior* (1924), *The Navigator* (1924), and *The General* (1926). He was known as **Old Stoneface** or the **Great Stoneface**.

›› Old Timber

In 1895 Henry Wood (1869–1944) founded the London Promenade Concerts (known as 'the Proms') and conducted these every year until his death. During this time Wood introduced British audiences to the music of such foreign composers as Schoenberg, Janáček, and Scriabin. His nickname **Old Timber** is an affectionate pun on his surname.

›› Ol' Man River

Ol' Man River, a name for the River Mississippi in North America, is the title of a song written by Jerome Kern and Oscar Hammerstein in 1927 for the musical *Showboat*: 'Dere's

an ol' man called de Mississippi;/ Dat's de ol' man dat I'd like
to be!/ ...But Ol' Man River,/ He jes' keeps rollin' along.'

▶▶ The One and Only

American Phyllis Dixey (1914–64) was the London West
End's first stripper. During the Second World War, she
brought her revue to the Whitehall Theatre. A 1978 TV movie
about her was titled *The One and Only Phyllis Dixey*.

▶▶ The Oomph Girl

The **Oomph Girl** was the US film actress Ann Sheridan
(1915–67). Early in her career her studio promoted her with
this tag, in a conscious echo of Clara Bow's **It Girl**, with the
word *oomph* similarly indicating sex appeal. Sheridan's films
include *Angels with Dirty Faces* (1938) and *King's Row* (1942).

▶▶ Orange Juice

O. J. Simpson. See ····▶ The **JUICE**.

▶▶ Our 'Enery

Henry Cooper (b.1934) was the British heavyweight
champion 1959–69 and 1970–71. He unsuccessfully
challenged Muhammad Ali for the world heavyweight title in
1966, after famously knocking down the American (then still
known as Cassius Clay) in 1963. Cooper's nickname **Our
'Enery** reveals his popularity with the British public and his
Cockney background. His powerful punch was known as
''Enery's 'Ammer'.

▶▶ Our Ginny

The English tennis player Virginia Wade (b.1945) was fondly
known in Britain as **Our Ginny**. Her singles titles include the
US Open (1968), the Australian Open (1972), and
Wimbledon (1977). This last victory, in the year of

Wimbledon's centenary and of Queen Elizabeth II's silver jubilee, cemented her place in the affections of the British public.

>> Our Gracie

In the 1930s Gracie Fields (1898–1979), the English singer and comedienne, starred in a series of popular films such as *Sally in Our Alley* (1931) and *Sing as We Go* (1934). Her broad Lancashire accent, cheerfulness, and humour made her hugely popular, particularly with working-class people, and she was said to be the world's highest paid entertainer by 1939. The affection with which she was regarded by the British public is demonstrated by her nickname **Our Gracie**.

>> Our Marie

Our Marie was Marie Lloyd (1870–1922), the English music-hall entertainer remembered for her risqué songs and flamboyant costumes. Among her most well-known songs are 'Oh! Mr Porter' and 'A Little of What You Fancy Does You Good'. As with Gracie Fields later, Marie Lloyd's nickname reflects the place she had in the British public's hearts. She was also known as the **Queen of the Halls**.

>> The Owls

Sheffield Wednesday football club's ground Hillsborough was originally known as Owlerton, hence their nickname the **Owls**. An owl appears on the club badge.

>> Oz

Recorded from the early 20th century, the informal name **Oz** is a phonetic representation of *Aus*, short for Australia.

▶▶ Paddy Pantsdown

The British politician Paddy Ashdown (b.1941) led the Liberal Democrats 1988–99. 'Paddy Pantsdown' was a *Sun* headline on 6 February 1992, following the disclosure of a brief affair Ashdown had had with his former secretary five years previously. Ashdown described the nickname in his diaries as 'dreadful — but brilliant'.

▶▶ Paddy's Wigwam

Paddy's Wigwam is a colourful nickname for the Roman Catholic Cathedral in Liverpool. It refers both to the distinctive shape of the cathedral's central lantern tower and to the city's large Irish Catholic population, Paddy being a nickname for an Irishman. The cathedral is also known as
····▶ the **MERSEY** Funnel.

▶▶ The Palmetto State

The flag of the US state of South Carolina bears the figure of a cabbage palmetto tree, a fan-leafed palm. The nickname the **Palmetto State** dates from around 1843.

▶▶ The Panhandle State

The term **Panhandle State** usually refers to West Virginia but is also sometimes applied to Idaho. A panhandle is a narrow strip of territory that projects into the territory of neighbouring states.

➤➤ Papa

The US writer Ernest Hemingway (1899–1961) had a tough, masculine image and was associated with such manly pursuits as big-game hunting, bullfighting, and deep-sea fishing. His friends, including Marlene Dietrich, used to call him **Papa**, a nickname that he seems to have coined himself. Hemingway's novels include *A Farewell to Arms* (1929), *For Whom the Bell Tolls* (1940), and *The Old Man and the Sea* (1952), and he was awarded the Nobel Prize for literature in 1954.

➤➤ Papa Doc

François Duvalier (1907–71) was President of Haiti 1957–71. Under a regime noted for being authoritarian and oppressive, many of his opponents were either executed without trial or forced into exile. Duvalier proclaimed himself President for life in 1964. Before entering politics he had trained as a physician, hence his nickname **Papa Doc**, the use of which he himself encouraged.

➤➤ Parrotface

With his beaky features and spluttering pronunciation, the British comedian Freddie Davies (b.1937) was a popular television performer in the 1960s and 1970s. He was nicknamed **Parrotface** or **Mr Parrotface**.

➤➤ La Pasionaria

During the Spanish Civil War (1936–39), Dolores Ibarruri (1895–1989) became famous as an inspirational leader of the Republicans, her emotional oratory winning her the nickname **La Pasionaria** (Spanish for 'passion-flower'). After Franco's victory, she went into exile in Moscow and didn't return to Spain until 1977. Margaret Thatcher was ironically described by the Labour politician Denis Healey as 'La Pasionaria of middle-class privilege'.

›› Paxo

Jeremy Paxman (b.1950) is best known for his tough,
confrontational style of interviewing politicians on the BBC
current affairs programme *Newsnight*. His nickname
obviously derives from his surname but, since it is also the
name of a brand of stuffing mix, also plays on the idea of his
unfortunate interviewees being 'stuffed' by Paxman.

›› The Peace Garden State

The International Peace Gardens in Bottineau, North Dakota,
are a landscaped park that crosses the northern border of the
state into the Canadian province of Manitoba. These
Gardens, which symbolize the friendship between Canada
and the United States, give North Dakota its nickname the
Peace Garden State.

›› The Peacemaker

Edward VII. See ····➤ **EDWARD** the Peacemaker.

›› The Peach State

The peach is the official state fruit of Georgia, hence the US
state's nickname the **Peach State**.

›› The Peekaboo Girl

Veronica Lake (1919–73) often played slinky femmes fatales in
1940s Hollywood thrillers. She was promoted as the **Peekaboo
Girl**, a reference to her distinctive peek-a-boo hairstyle in which
her long blonde hair was draped over one eye. This style was
much imitated by female film-goers of the time.

›› The Pelican State

The pelican is the official state bird of Louisiana, the **Pelican
State**, and has been depicted on the state seal since before the
Civil War. The birds are plentiful along the state's Gulf coast.

❯❯ The People's Princess

The **People's Princess** was an informal name for Diana, Princess of Wales (1961–97) popularized by Tony Blair on hearing of her death: 'She was the People's Princess, and that is how she will stay...in our hearts and in our memories forever.' It was the journalist Julie Burchill who originally used this phrase to describe the princess.

❯❯ Perfidious Albion

Perfidious Albion translates the French phrase *la perfide Albion* and is sometimes used to describe England or Britain by those who suspect the country of being treacherous in international affairs. The phrase is said to have been coined by the Marquis de Ximenès (1726–1817) and was in widespread use by the end of the Napoleonic War. Both terms are recorded in English from the mid 19th century. Albion is a poetic or literary term for England or Britain, probably of Celtic origin and related to Latin *albus* ('white'), referring to the white cliffs of Dover.

❯❯ Phil the Greek

Prince Philip, the Duke of Edinburgh (b.1921), is the son of Prince Andrew of Greece and Denmark. Although his ancestry is Danish rather than Greek, Prince Philip is nevertheless sometimes disrespectfully referred to as **Phil the Greek**.

❯❯ Phoenix City

The US city of Chicago, Illinois was dubbed **Phoenix City** by Henry Ward Beecher after its recovery from the disastrous fire of 1871.

❯❯ Phoney Quid

British admiral Dudley Pound (1877–1943) was Commander-in-Chief of the Mediterranean fleet (1936–39) and in 1939 he became Admiral of the Fleet and First Sea Lord. He was generally known as Dud Pound, which was sometimes humorously paraphrased as **Phoney Quid**.

›› The Phrasemaker

Woodrow Wilson (1856–1924), President of the US 1913–21, brought the US into the First World War in 1917 and was later instrumental in the formation of the League of Nations. The **Phrasemaker**, as he was called, had a gift for oratory and for such memorable phrases as 'The world must be made safe for democracy', used when addressing Congress in 1917 to ask for a declaration of war against Germany.

›› Pig Island

In the late 19th and early 20th centuries, Australians referred to New Zealand as **Pig Island**, because of the large numbers of wild pigs in rural parts of the country, descended from the pigs originally brought by Captain James Cook.

›› Pincher

British admiral William Fanshawe Martin (1801–95) was a strict disciplinarian, noted for having ratings 'pinched', or arrested, for minor offences. He became known as **Pincher** Martin and, in naval and military circles, Pincher subsequently became the inevitable nickname of any man surnamed Martin.

›› The Pine Tree State

The US state of Maine has been known as the **Pine Tree State** since the mid 19th century. Four-fifths of the state is forested, mainly with pine trees. A pine tree appears on the state seal.

›› Pistol Pete[1]

The original **Pistol Pete** was the basketball player Pete Maravich (1947–88). A prolific scorer and on-court

showman, Maravich became college basketball's all-time high
scorer while playing for Louisiana State University. He started
his NBA career in 1970 with the Atlanta Hawks, later playing
for the New Orleans Jazz and the Boston Celtics.

❱❱ Pistol Pete[2]

In 2002 US tennis player Pete Sampras (b.1971) won the
US Open, his 14th Grand Slam tournament. He had
previously won the US title four times, the Australian twice,
and Wimbledon seven times. In 1993 he became the first
player to serve over 1000 aces in a season, his powerful,
often unreturnable, serves earning him his nickname **Pistol
Pete**.

❱❱ The Platinum Blonde

Hollywood's **Platinum Blonde** was Jean Harlow (1911–37),
whose films include one with that title (1931). The term can
also be used to describe any woman with pale silvery-blonde
hair.

❱❱ The Plymouth of the West

The US city of San Diego, California, was one of the first
settlements on the West Coast, founded in 1769 by Father
Junípero Serra. Its nickname the **Plymouth of the West** is a
reference to Plymouth, Massachusetts, where the Pilgrim
Fathers settled in 1620.

❱❱ The Pocket Dictator

Engelbert Dollfuss (1892–1934), Chancellor of Austria
1932–34, attempted to block Austrian Nazi plans to force
the *Anschluss* by suppressing Parliament and governing by
decree. He was known as the **Pocket Dictator** because of
his small stature. Dollfuss was assassinated by Austrian
Nazis.

➤➤ Pompey

Pompey is a nickname for the town and dockyard of Portsmouth, England. This appears to be naval slang, dating back to the late 19th century, but its origin remains obscure. It is also the nickname of Portsmouth Football Club, as heard in the old chant 'Play up Pompey, Pompey play up!'.

➤➤ The Pond

The North Atlantic Ocean. See ••••➤ The **HERRING** Pond.

➤➤ The Poor Little Rich Girl

Barbara Hutton (1912–79), the US heiress to the Woolworth fortune, inherited $10 million when she was 21. But wealth didn't bring her happiness. Married seven times, she had a life beset by troubles, partly through ill health. The press dubbed her **Poor Little Rich Girl**, after the title of a song by Noël Coward (1925). When Hutton married the film actor Cary Grant in 1947, the couple were nicknamed **Cash and Cary**.

➤➤ The Pope

At the age of 25 Enrico Fermi (1901–54) was appointed professor of theoretical physics at the University of Rome. His students there nicknamed him the **Pope** because they thought he was infallible. The Italian-born US atomic physicist was awarded the Nobel Prize for physics in 1938. Fermi directed the first controlled nuclear chain reaction in 1942.

➤➤ The Pope of Trash

Film-maker John Waters (b.1946) is notorious for the wilful bad taste of his movies, reflecting his fascination with kitsch, sex, and bodily functions. These include *Mondo Trasho* (1969), *Pink Flamingos* (1972), *Hairspray* (1988), and

Cecil B. Demented (2000). *Pink Flamingos* was described by *Variety* as 'one of the most vile, stupid, and repulsive films ever made'. His nickname the **Pope of Trash** was coined by the writer William S. Burroughs. Waters has also been described as the **Prince of Puke** and the **Sultan of Sleaze**.

›› Poppy

George Bush (b.1924) was President of the US 1989–93. **Poppy** is a family nickname from his boyhood that stayed with him into adult life. His uncles used to call his father Pop and began calling George Little Pop, later shortened to Poppy.

›› Pops

Pops is a term of address popular among black jazz musicians and usually (though not invariably) applied to someone older than the speaker. Louis Armstrong frequently used the term and was often affectionately addressed as such himself. The band-leader Paul Whiteman was also known as Pops by his musicians.

›› Popski's Private Army

Popski's Private Army was a unit of the Long-Range Desert Patrol, a British military force formed in 1942 to carry out reconnaissance and sabotage behind enemy lines in North Africa during the Second World War. The unit was led by Lieutenant Colonel Vladimir Peniakoff (1897–1951), a Russian-born Belgian serving with the British army and familiarly known as **Popski** because it was easier to pronounce.

›› Posh

As a member of the Spice Girls pop group in the 1990s, Victoria Adams (b.1975) was nicknamed **Posh Spice**. The other members of the group were known as **Baby Spice**,

Ginger Spice, **Scary Spice**, and **Sporty Spice**. Each of these nicknames was designed to reflect the character of the singer it was applied to; in Adams's case it referred to her unsmiling, slightly haughty on-stage demeanour. Later known simply as **Posh**, she married the footballer David Beckham in 1999, the celebrity couple becoming known in the newspapers as **Posh 'n' Becks**. When in 2002–03 the football club Peterborough United, itself nicknamed the **Posh**, applied to register the nickname as a trademark, Victoria Beckham was reported to have contested the club's right to do so.

›› The Posh

When Peterborough United football club was formed in 1934, the fans were promised 'posh players for a posh new team'. Peterborough United has been known as the **Posh** ever since.

›› The Potters

The area around Stoke-on-Trent, Staffordshire, where the English pottery industry is based, is known as the Potteries. Stoke City football club is accordingly nicknamed the **Potters**.

›› The Power

Darts player Phil Taylor's (b.1960) nickname the **Power** reflects his worldwide dominance of the sport since the mid-1990s. In 2004 he won his eleventh World Darts Championship title.

›› The Prairie State

Although the Prairie States has been used as a collective term for the states of Illinois, Wisconsin, Iowa, Minnesota, and others to the south, it is Illinois with which the nickname the **Prairie State** has generally been associated since the mid 19th century.

175   *Prez*

›› The Prefect

Malcolm Fraser (b.1930), Prime Minister of Australia 1975–83, was known as the **Prefect** because of his earnest and somewhat dictatorial style of leadership. In 1985 Fraser represented Australia in a Commonwealth group formed to negotiate the peaceful dismantling of South Africa's apartheid policy.

›› The Premier State

New South Wales was the first Australian state to be founded, hence its nickname the **Premier State**.

›› The President

Lester Young. See ····➤ **PREZ**.

›› The Preston Plumber

The **Preston Plumber** was the affectionate nickname for the English footballer Tom Finney (b.1922). Finney was genuinely two-footed and could play anywhere in the forward line. For the whole of his career he played for his home-town club Preston North End, scoring 187 goals. He also won 76 international caps, scoring 30 goals for England. Before starting his football career Finney worked as a plumber, later running his own business.

›› Pretty Boy Floyd

US bankrobber Charles Arthur Floyd (1904–34) probably acquired his nickname **Pretty Boy Floyd** in a Kansas City brothel. It was a name he hated and he is said to have killed at least two fellow gangsters who called him this. Floyd himself was shot and killed by FBI agents in Ohio in 1934.

›› Prez

The jazz saxophonist Lester Young (1909–59) started

working as an accompanist for the singer Billie Holiday in the late 1930s. Once he had coined her nickname ····▶ **LADY** Day, Holiday returned the compliment by calling him **President**, later shortened to **Prez** (or **Pres**). She is said to have been admiringly comparing the saxophonist to the then President Franklin Roosevelt.

▶▶ Prezza

John Prescott (b.1938), the British politician, was made deputy prime minister in 1997. He is sometimes called **Prezza**, a version of his surname styled on nicknames such as **Gazza** and **Hezza**.

▶▶ The Prime Minister of Mirth

From the 1890s, George Robey (1869–1954) performed in music halls, originally singing humorous songs and later developing comic characters to perform in sketches. Billed the **Prime Minister of Mirth**, Robey was typically dressed in a long black coat and bowler hat, with two thickly-painted black eyebrows. He later acted in Shakespeare, playing Falstaff on stage and appearing in Laurence Olivier's film *Henry V* (1944).

▶▶ The Prince of Darkness[1]

Johnny Carson (b.1925) became known as the **Prince of Darkness** for dominating late-night US television for 30 years. From 1962 he hosted *The Tonight Show*, a chat show broadcast every night from 11.30 to 12.30 and attracting huge audiences. He was noted for his quick wit and satirical commentary on current affairs.

▶▶ The Prince of Darkness[2]

Peter Mandelson (b.1953), the British Labour politician, is sometimes called the **Prince of Darkness**, a reference to his perceived mastery of the 'black art' of spin-doctoring. The phrase was originally a name for the Devil, recorded from the early 17th century. Mandelson is also known as the **Sultan of Spin**.

❯❯ The Prince of Wails

In the 1950s, the US pop singer Johnnie Ray (1927–90) was noted for his tearful rendition of such songs as 'Cry' and 'The Little White Cloud That Cried', the double-sided single that was no. 1 for eleven weeks in 1952. He earned several nicknames including the **Prince of Wails**, the **Nabob of Sob**, and the **Cry Guy**.

❯❯ The Prisoner of Spandau

In 1941, Rudolf Hess (1894–1987), deputy leader of the Nazi Party, secretly parachuted into Scotland in a bid to negotiate peace terms with Britain. He was imprisoned for the duration of the war and, at the Nuremberg trials, sentenced to life imprisonment in Spandau prison, Berlin, for war crimes. From 1966 until his death in 1987 he was the only inmate of Spandau.

❯❯ The Prof

During the Second World War, Lord Cherwell, Frederick Lindemann (1886–1957), was Winston Churchill's personal adviser on scientific and aeronautical matters. The German-born British physicist was Professor of Experimental Philosophy at Oxford (1919–56) and director of the Clarendon Laboratory. He was widely known as the **Prof**, a nickname he apparently first came by at the house of Lord Birkenhead around 1920.

❯❯ The Professor[1]

Woodrow Wilson (1856–1924) was President of the US 1913–21. A prominent academic prior to his election victory, Wilson had been a professor of law and politics at Princeton

University. His academic background, and the scholarly
manner he exhibited in political life, earned him the
nicknames the **Professor** and the **Schoolmaster**.

▶▶ The Professor[2]

With his trademark handlebar moustache, the comedian
Jimmy Edwards (1920–88) is best remembered playing the
bullying, blustering headmaster of a minor public school in
the British TV series *Whacko!* (1956–60, 1971–72). His
character was called Professor Jimmy Edwards. It was for
playing such academic roles (and his Cambridge education)
that he was nicknamed the **Professor**.

▶▶ Psycho

Nicknamed **Psycho** because of his crunching tackling, the
footballer Stuart Pearce (b.1962) won 78 caps for England
and played for a number of clubs including Nottingham
Forest and Manchester City.

▶▶ Public Enemy No. 1

John Dillinger (1903–34) was a notorious bank robber and
murderer who in 1933 became the first wanted criminal to be
named the FBI's **Public Enemy No. 1** by the US Attorney
General, Homer Cummings. He was shot and killed by FBI
agents in Chicago in 1934.

▶▶ The Puke State

The US state of Missouri was formerly known as the **Puke
State**. It has been suggested that this may be a corruption of
Pikes, a word used in California to refer to white migratory
workers from Pike County, Missouri.

▶▶ Pussyfoot Johnson

W. E. Johnson (1862–1945) was nicknamed **Pussyfoot
Johnson** because of his stealthy methods pursuing criminals

as a special officer in the US Indian Service (1908–11) in
Indian Territory. Johnson later campaigned for the
prohibitionist cause in the US and tirelessly lectured on
temperance all over Europe. The term *pussyfoot*, meaning an
advocate of prohibition or a teetotaller, derived from
Johnson's nickname.

▶▶ Quaker City

The US city of Philadelphia, Pennsylvania, was founded in 1682 by William Penn (1644–1718) as a Quaker colony, hence its nickname **Quaker City**.

▶▶ The Quakers

Darlington football club became known as the **Quakers** because its ground Feethams was originally owned by the prominent local Quaker and slavery abolitionist John Beaumont Pease. A Quaker hat appears on the club's badge.

▶▶ The Quaker State

The US state of Pennsylvania is named after the father of its founder, William Penn (1644–1718). Penn was granted a charter to land in North America by Charles II and used it to found the colony of Pennsylvania as a sanctuary for persecuted Quakers and other Nonconformists in 1682. As a result Pennsylvania is sometimes called the **Quaker State**.

▶▶ The Queen of Burlesque

In the 1930s, Gypsy Rose Lee (1914–70) became famous on Broadway for her striptease act, which raised what was previously considered a sleazy form of entertainment to a stylish and sophisticated art. Billed as the **Queen of Burlesque**, she found herself fêted by the New York intellectual set, including Damon Runyon.

›› The Queen of Crime

Two English writers of detective fiction have been hailed as the **Queen of Crime**, first Agatha Christie (1890–1976), then her successor P. D. James (b.1920). Many of Christie's novels feature the Belgian Hercule Poirot or the resourceful Miss Marple, her two most famous creations. Among her best-known detective stories are *Murder on the Orient Express* (1934) and *Death on the Nile* (1937). James is noted for her novels featuring the poet-detective Adam Dalgleish, including *Death of an Expert Witness* (1977) and *A Taste for Death* (1986).

›› The Queen of Hearts

The title the **Queen of Hearts** was applied to Diana, Princess of Wales, following an interview she gave on the

10. *The Queen of Hearts*

BBC TV programme *Panorama* in 1995: 'I'd like to be a queen in people's hearts but I don't see myself being Queen of this country.' The term came to be frequently used by the newspapers in connection with Diana's charity work.

>> The Queen of the Antilles

The **Queen of the Antilles** is Cuba. The Antilles are the group of islands that form the greater part of the West Indies, of which Cuba is the largest.

>> The Queen of the Blues

Although Dinah Washington (1924–63) was not exclusively a blues singer, her feeling for that music earned her the title the **Queen of the Blues**. Noted for her husky voice and unique phrasing, she also sang gospel, jazz, rhythm-and-blues and pop, having notable hits with such recordings as 'What a Diff'rence a Day Makes' and 'Our Love is Here to Stay'.

>> The Queen of the Halls

Marie Lloyd. See ····➤ **OUR** Marie.

>> The Queen State

The US state of Maryland is named after Queen Henrietta Maria, wife of Charles I, and is sometimes known as the **Queen State**.

>> Queer Hardie

Keir Hardie (1856–1915) was the first leader of both the Independent Labour Party (1893) and the Labour Party (1906). Although he remained an MP until his death, his pacifism isolated him from his Labour colleagues during the First World War. His nickname **Queer Hardie** comes from his idiosyncrasies, such as wearing a cloth cap.

>> The Quiet Man

Iain Duncan Smith (b.1954) became leader of the
Conservative Party in 2001. Criticized for his lack of
charisma, Duncan Smith declared at the following year's
party conference: 'Do not underestimate the determination of
a quiet man'. This prompted Labour MPs to greet the Tory
leader with a loud and prolonged 'Shhh' whenever he stood
up to speak in the House of Commons. In 2003, again at the
party conference, Duncan Smith announced: 'The quiet man
is here to stay and he is turning up the volume.' A few weeks
later he was replaced as party leader by Michael Howard.

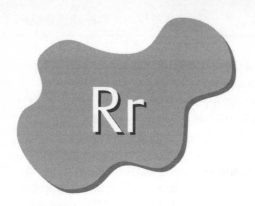

❯❯ Rab

Richard Austen Butler (1902–82), the British Conservative politician, was universally known as **Rab** Butler, from his initials. As Minister of Education (1941–45) he was responsible for the Education Act (1944), which introduced free primary and secondary education for all. Butler was twice an unsuccessful candidate for the leadership of the Conservative Party. The team of younger Conservatives who worked under Butler to reform the party after its 1945 election defeat were known as 'Rab's Boys'.

❯❯ Rabbit

Jazz alto saxophonist Johnny Hodges (1906–70), who played with Duke Ellington's band for nearly 40 years, was known as **Rabbit**. This probably came from his taste for lettuce and tomato sandwiches. An alternative explanation has been mooted, though. It may have been a reference to an occasion when the musician was said to have made frequent visits to the rooms of a brothel. Hodges' other nickname was **Jeep**.

❯❯ The Rag (and Famish)

The Army and Navy Club in London, familiarly known as the **Rag**, was founded in 1837. The nickname is first recorded in Trollope's novel *The Three Clerks* (1858). It is said to have been coined by a Captain William Duff of the 23rd Fusiliers, when he referred to the food offered when he arrived for supper late one night as a mere 'rag and famish affair'. This was an allusion to the 'Rag and Famish', a cheap local gaming-house and brothel.

➤➤ The Ragin' Cajun

James Carville (b.1944) was Bill Clinton's fiery political strategist, best known for being chief strategist on Clinton's 1992 presidential campaign. A native of Louisiana with a heavy southern accent, he picked up his nickname the **Ragin' Cajun** while running Lloyd Doggett's unsuccessful bid for the governorship of Texas in 1983.

➤➤ The Rajah

Rogers Hornsby (1896–1963), known as the **Rajah** because of his aura of almost regal command, played baseball with the St Louis Cardinals and Chicago Cubs. Acknowledged as one of the game's greatest hitters, his career batting average of 0.358 is second only to Ty Cobb.

➤➤ The Rams

Derby County football club takes its nickname the **Rams** from the famous breed of Derbyshire rams.

➤➤ The Rand

Witwatersrand is a goldfield district near Johannesburg, South Africa. From its informal name, the **Rand**, came the name *rand* for the base monetary unit of South Africa. Another nickname for Witwatersrand is the **Reef**.

➤➤ Ranji

K. S. Ranjitsinhji Vibhaji (1872–1933), the Indian cricketer known as **Ranji** for short, made his debut for Sussex in 1895, and scored a total of 72 centuries as a batsman for Sussex and England. In 1907 he succeeded his cousin as Maharaja of the state of Navanagar.

➤➤ The Rawalpindi Express

Born in Rawalpindi, Pakistan, Shoaib Akhtar (b.1975) is a fast bowler of blistering speed, hence his nickname the **Rawalpindi Express**. It has inspired many newspaper headlines on the lines of 'Aussies derailed by Rawalpindi Express'. In 2002 Shoaib bowled the first ever 100mph delivery, during a one-day international between Pakistan and New Zealand.

Ronald Reagan

Ronald Reagan was known by a number of nicknames during his presidency:

Dutch — childhood nickname, from his father's remark 'For such a little bit of a fat Dutchman, he makes a hell of a lot of noise'

the Gipper — from the nickname of the American footballer George Gipp, a role the former film actor played in a film. Reagan would later urge his supporters to 'win one for the Gipper'

the Great Communicator — reference to Reagan's folksy, conversational way of addressing the American people and his effective use of television and radio

Old Hopalong — British nickname for the president and former actor in Hollywood westerns, after the cowboy character Hopalong Cassidy

the Teflon President — because, whatever blunders or scandals he was prone to, nothing seemed to stick

❯❯ The Red Baron

Manfred, Baron von Richthofen (1882–1918), the German
fighter pilot, shot down 80 enemy aircraft, making him the
leading fighter ace of the First World War. His nickname the
Red Baron derived not only from his aristocratic title but also
from the distinctive bright red aircraft he flew. Richthofen
was eventually shot down himself, either by a Canadian ace
flying with the RAF or by Australian small-arms fire from the
ground.

❯❯ The Red Dean

Hewlett Johnson (1874–1966) was Dean of Canterbury
1931–63. Newspapers dubbed him the **Red Dean** because of
his controversial Communist sympathies. He visited both the
Soviet Union and China.

Red Heads

Among the many nicknames for redheads are **Beetroot**, **Brick
Top**, **Carrot Top**, **Carrots**, **Copper Top**, **Ginger**, **Gingernut**,
Red, and **Rusty**. In Australia red-haired men are sometimes
called **Bluey**. The Norse explorer Eric the **Red**, was
so-named because he had red hair, as did the Italian
composer Antonio Vivaldi, the **Red Priest**. Other famous
Reds include the film actor Red Buttons, the comedian Red
Skelton, the jazz trumpeter Red Allen, and the oil-well
firefighter Red Adair. The two best-known **Gingers** are
probably the film actress and dancer Ginger Rogers and the
rock drummer Ginger Baker.

▶▶ Red Ellen

Ellen Wilkinson (1891–1947) served as Labour MP for
Jarrow 1935–47 and was appointed Minister of Education in
1945, the first woman to hold such a position. Red-haired
and a former member of the Communist Party, she was
popularly known as **Red Ellen**.

▶▶ Red Ken

Ken Livingstone (b.1945) was the leader of the Greater
London Council 1981–86 and MP for Brent East 1987–2001.
His outspoken left-wing views as leader of the GLC earned
him the nickname **Red Ken** in the right-wing press, for whom
he became something of a hate figure. Livingstone was
elected mayor of London in 2000.

▶▶ The Reef

Witwatersrand. See ····▶ The **RAND**.

▶▶ The Refrigerator

William Perry (b.1962), the US American football player
who played for the Chicago Bears, was known as the
Refrigerator. This was partly because he was said to be able
to eat the contents of a fridge and partly because of his
330lb (150kg) bulk. Another sporting figure compared to a
fridge, but for a different reason, was Chris Evert,
····▶ **MISS** Frigidaire.

▶▶ The Robins

Cheltenham Town football club, founded in 1892, originally
played in deep red shirts and were nicknamed the **Rubies**. In
the 1930s they changed to a red-and-white strip and adopted
the nickname the **Robins**. The nickname is shared by Bristol
City, Swindon Town, and Wrexham.

›› Robocop

As Detective Superintendent of Cleveland police in the
1990s, Ray Mallon (b.1955) introduced 'zero-tolerance'
policing, in which burglars and anti-social behaviour were
vigorously targeted. He was dubbed **Robocop** by the press
after the remorseless crime-fighting cyborg in the 1987
science-fiction film of that title. Mallon was elected mayor of
Middlesbrough in 2002.

›› The Rock

An informal name for Gibraltar is the **Rock**. The British
dependency is situated at the foot of the Rock of Gibraltar, a
rocky headland at the southern tip of Spain. Alcatraz, a rocky
island in San Francisco Bay, California, which was the site of
a top-security federal prison between 1934 and 1963, was
also known as the **Rock**.

›› The Rocket[1]

Born in Rockhampton, Queensland, the Australian tennis
player Rod Laver (b.1938) was known as the **Rocket** or the
Rockhampton Rocket because of the power with which he
hit the ball. When Laver was still a teenager, the tag was
coined by the Australian tennis coach Harry Hopman. Laver
was the only player twice to win the four major singles
championships (British, American, French, and Australian) in
one year, first in 1962 and then in 1969. In all he won 11
Grand Slam titles.

›› The Rocket[2]

In baseball, the **Rocket** was Roger Clemens (b.1962), a
pitcher with the Boston Red Sox. He was so called because of
his powerful build and the speed of his deliveries.

›› The Rough Rider

Theodore Roosevelt (1858–1919) was President of the US 1901–9. During the Spanish–American War of 1898, Roosevelt had raised and commanded a volunteer cavalry force that became known as the Rough Riders. The name later came to be applied to Roosevelt himself, celebrating his status as a war hero.

›› Safe Hands

Safe Hands is the self-coined nickname of the former England goalkeeper David Seaman (b.1963). It is how he signs autographs and is also the title of his autobiography (2000). Seaman, who enjoyed great success playing for Arsenal (1990–2003), won 75 international caps.

›› The Sagebrush State

The **Sagebrush State** is Nevada. The sagebrush is a shrubby aromatic North American plant of the daisy family which is abundant in the arid state of Nevada. It is the state's official flower and gives Nevada its nickname.

›› St Mugg

Malcolm Muggeridge (1903–90), the British journalist, writer, and broadcaster, often explored spiritual and religious issues on television, at first from a sceptical perspective. Following his conversion to Roman Catholicism in 1982, he earned his somewhat ironic nickname **St Mugg**.

›› The Saints

Southampton football club are nicknamed the **Saints**, which stems from the club's formation in 1885. The team was originally named Southampton St Mary's, since many of the founding players were members of St Mary's Church YMCA.

The connection with the church remained strong in the club's early years; indeed, its first president was the Reverend A. B. Sole, curate of St Mary's. This link has been re-established in recent years with the club's move to its new stadium St Mary's.

›› Sally Army

The Salvation Army is an international Christian organization for evangelistic and social work among the poor and destitute, founded in 1865 by William Booth and given its present name in 1878. The organization is affectionately known as the **Sally Army** (or the **Sally Ann**). This use of **Sally** dates back to the early 20th century.

›› The Sandlapper State

South Carolina's nickname the **Sandlapper State** is said to refer to some of its early settlers who lived on barren sand ridges in such poverty and hardship that they were forced to eat sand in order to survive.

›› Sarah Heartburn

Sarah Bernhardt (1844–1923), the great French actress, was humorously known as **Sarah Heartburn**, a playful reversal of her surname.

›› Satchmo

Louis Armstrong (1900–71) is celebrated for his brilliant jazz trumpet playing and distinctive gravelly voice. Armstrong's most popular nickname came from the slang term *satchel-mouth*, i.e. a person with a big mouth. He sometimes referred to his trumpet too as Satchelmouth. The abbreviated form **Satchmo**, later itself shortened to **Satch**, seems to date from around 1932. According to Armstrong, the first person to address him as Satchmo was the editor of *Melody Maker*, Percy Mathison Brooks.

❯❯ The Say Hey Kid

Willie Mays (b.1931) was a star baseball player for the
New York Giants and San Francisco Giants. A great
centerfielder, he hit 660 home runs during his 22-year
career (1951–73). Mays became known as the **Say Hey Kid**
at the start of his career because he could never remember
other players' names. To catch their attention he would shout
'Say, hey!'

❯❯ Scarface

Al Capone (1899–1947) was heavily involved in organized
crime in Chicago in the 1920s and controlled a vast
bootlegging empire. His nickname **Scarface**, or **Scarface Al**,
which Capone himself detested, derived from a huge scar on
his left cheek. This was the result of a razor slash he
received in a Brooklyn gang fight in his youth. He was
eventually imprisoned in 1931 for federal income tax
evasion.

❯❯ Schnozzola

After a long career in vaudeville, night clubs, and films,
Jimmy Durante (1893–1980) successfully moved into
television in the 1950s. The US comedian and entertainer
was popularly known as **Schnozzola** (or **Schnozzle**) because
of his big nose. *Schnozz* or *schnozzle* is US slang for the nose,
from a Yiddish word deriving from the German word
Schnauze meaning a snout.

❯❯ Scu

Peter Scudamore (b.1958) was champion jockey from 1986
to 1992 and in the 1988–89 season he rode a record 221
winners. By his retirement in 1993 he had ridden a total of
1,678 winners. He was known as **Scu**, a shortening of his
surname.

» The Scud

The Australian tennis player Mark Philippoussis (b.1976),
noted for his blistering serve, is nicknamed the **Scud**, after a
type of long-range guided missile. The nickname has helped
headline-writers avoid using the player's long surname in
headlines such as *Scud grounded* or *Scud launches at
Wimbledon*.

» Shagger Norris

The British Conservative politician Steven Norris
(b.1945) picked up the tabloid nickname **Shagger Norris** in
1993 while he was a transport minister, following
revelations in the press of several mistresses. Norris was an
unsuccessful candidate in the 2000 election for mayor of
London.

» The Shakers

One of the Bury football club's first chairmen predicted that
his team would give a rival team 'a good shaking', hence the
nickname they acquired, the **Shakers**.

» Shanks

Bill Shankly (1913–81) managed Liverpool FC for 15 years
(1959–74), during which period the club won three league
championships, two FA Cup finals, and one UEFA Cup. He
was affectionately known as **Shanks**.

» Shaq

At 7ft 1in (216cm), Shaquille O'Neal (b.1972), known as
Shaq, towers over a basketball court and is thought by many
to be the most dominant player in the game since Michael
Jordan. He led his team the Los Angeles Lakers to NBA Finals
victories in 2000, 2001, and 2002.

❯❯ The Shoe

US jockey Willie Shoemaker (1931–2003), universally known as the **Shoe**, rode 8,833 winners during his long career, which lasted from 1949 to 1990. At the age of 54, he became in 1986 the oldest jockey to win the Kentucky Derby, a race he first won 32 years previously. He was the first jockey to reach $100 million in earnings.

❯❯ Shoeless Joe

Joe Jackson (1889–1951), known as **Shoeless Joe**, was one of the great hitters in the history of baseball. His nickname came about after he once played a minor league game in his stocking feet because a new pair of spikes he was breaking in had given him blisters. Jackson was banned from the sport for his involvement in the 1919 'Black Sox' scandal, in which Jackson and seven other Chicago White Sox players were bribed to throw the 1919 World Series. After Jackson gave his testimony at the ensuing trial, a tearful boy is said to have approached his idol and implored him to 'Say it ain't so, Joe'.

❯❯ The Show Me State

The US state of Missouri is known as the **Show Me State**. 'Show Me' here refers to what was regarded as the characteristically sceptical approach of the people of Missouri. In 1902 Willard D. Vandiner, a former Congressman from Columbia, Missouri, is supposed to have said 'I'm from Missouri, and you've got to show me'.

❯❯ The Shrimp

Jean Shrimpton (b.1942) was an English fashion model of the 1960s who helped to introduce the miniskirt. She was nicknamed the **Shrimp**, an abbreviation of her surname that fitted her slight figure.

Short

Nicknames for a person of small stature include **Half Pint**, **Munchkin**, **Nipper**, **Short Stuff**, **Shortly**, **Pee-Wee** (in the US), and **Titch**. Some historical shorties are **Curthose**, meaning 'Short Boot' (Robert II, Duke of Normandy); the **Little Corporal** (Napoleon Bonaparte); the **Little Magician** (US president Martin van Buren); and the **Little Wonder** (prizefighter Tom Sayers). Nicknames of famously diminutive people who appear in this book include **Little Mo** (Maureen Connolly); **Little Sparrow** (Edith Piaf); **Mighty Mouse** (Kevin Keegan); the **Toy Bulldog** (Mickey Walker); and **Wee Willie** (Willie Keeler).

›› Sicknote

The English footballer Darren Anderton (b.1972) has been injury-prone during his career, missing many games for his club, hence the nickname he's been given by exasperated Tottenham Hotspur supporters. A sick note is a note given to an employer or teacher explaining a person's absence due to illness.

›› Silent Cal

Calvin Coolidge (1872–1933), 30th President of the US 1923–29, was famous for the brevity of his public utterances, his economy with words earning him the nickname **Silent Cal**. In the summer of 1927 he announced abruptly 'I do not choose to run for president in 1928.' When his death was

announced, humorist Dorothy Parker is said to have
remarked, 'How could they tell?'

›› Silicon Valley

The term **Silicon...** is used to denote an area with a high
concentration of computing and electronics companies or
industries. The most famous such name is **Silicon Valley**, an
area between San José and Palo Alto in Santa Clara County
south-east of San Francisco, California. On the same model,
there is a so-called **Silicon Glen** in central lowland Scotland, a
Silicon Fen in Cambridge, a **Silicon Prairie** near Dallas, Texas,
and a **Silicon Alley** in New York.

›› The Silver State

The discovery of silver in Nevada in 1858 led to the rapid
growth of silver mining in the state, hence its nickname the
Silver State.

Frank Sinatra

Frank Sinatra's various nicknames chart the course of his career:

Bones — so-called by the other musicians when he was a skinny
singer with Tommy Dorsey's band in the late 1930s

the Voice — his billing as a solo star in the 1940s and the title of
one of his earliest albums

the Chairman of the Board, **the Gov'nor**, **the Pope** — all
nicknames for Sinatra in the early 1960s, when he led the 'Rat
Pack', a group of Las Vegas-based entertainers including Dean
Martin, Sammy Davis Jr, Peter Lawford, and Joey Bishop

Ol' Blue Eyes — what he was affectionately called in the later
part of his career, following his post-retirement comeback in
1973 with the album *Ol' Blue Eyes is Back*

➤➤ The Singer's Singer

Two US singers have received the accolade the **Singer's Singer**, Tony Bennett and Mel Tormé. Tony Bennett (b.1926) is the jazz-influenced singer of pop ballads such as 'I Left My Heart in San Francisco' (1962) whom Frank Sinatra called 'the best singer in the business'. Mel Tormé (1925–99) was the much-admired crooner of the late 1940s and 1950s.

➤➤ The Singing Capon

Nelson Eddy. See ····➤ The IRON Butterfly.

➤➤ The Singing Cowboy

Two US film actors were known as the **Singing Cowboy**, Roy Rogers and Gene Autry. Roy Rogers (1912–98) starred and sang in many B-film westerns of the 1930s and 1940s, accompanied by his horse Trigger. Gene Autrey (1907–98), with his horse Champion, replaced Rogers as cinema's most popular singing cowboy, before moving to television in the 1950s.

➤➤ Singing Indurain

Miguel Indurain (b.1964) was only the fourth cyclist to win the Tour de France five times (1991–95). The Spaniard's nickname was **Singing Indurain**, a delightful pun on the title of the Gene Kelly musical *Singin' in the Rain* (1952).

➤➤ The Sioux State

The US state of North Dakota is sometimes called the **Sioux State**. This refers to the Sioux, a North American Indian people, also known as the Dakota (meaning 'allies'), who once occupied the plains and prairies of the territory.

➤➤ Sir Geoffrey

Geoffrey Boycott. See ····➤ BOYCS.

➤➤ Sir Shortly Floorcross

The British politician Sir Hartley Shawcross (1902–2003)
served as Attorney-General 1945–51 in the Labour government
but resigned from the party in 1958, earning himself the
ingenious nickname **Sir Shortly Floorcross**. In the British House
of Commons, to 'cross the floor' is to change one's party
allegiance, literally by moving across the *floor* or open space
which divides the Government and the Opposition benches.

➤➤ Skeeter

Wilma Rudolph (1940–94) won three sprint gold medals for
the US at the 1960 Olympics, in the 100m, 200m and relay.
Her nickname **Skeeter** (US slang for a mosquito) was coined
by her high school basketball coach Clinton Gray who told
her, 'You're little and fast and you always get in my way'.
Rudolph was born with polio and at the age of four she
contracted double pneumonia and scarlet fever
simultaneously. For a time she was unable to use her left leg
and had to wear a leg brace until she was eight.

➤➤ Skeets

Between 1978 and 1981, Renaldo Nehemiah (b.1959) was
the finest high hurdler in the world, but in 1982 joined the
San Francisco 49ers to begin a career in professional football.
He returned to the track in 1986. He was known as **Skeets**,
like Wilma Rudolph's nickname **Skeeter**, a slang term in
American English for a mosquito.

➤➤ Slick Willy

Prior to his time as US president, Bill Clinton (b.1946) served
five terms as Governor of Arkansas 1979–81 and 1983–92.
Clinton's enemies in Arkansas, who accused him of dubious
political tactics and evasiveness, gave him the nickname **Slick
Willy**. The label is thought to have been coined by John
Robert Starr, editor of the *Arkansas Democrat*.

›› Sly

Sylvester Stallone. See ••••➤ The **ITALIAN** Stallion.

›› Smack

Fletcher Henderson (1898–1952) was a jazz pianist,
composer, arranger, and bandleader. He introduced the idea
of the big band divided into brass, reed, and rhythm sections
and his arrangements, many of which were used by Benny
Goodman's band, were enormously influential on the sound
of the swing era. Henderson's nickname **Smack** was
apparently from the smacking sound he made with his lips.
There does not seem to be any connection with the slang use
of the term to mean heroin.

›› The Smoke

London. See ••••➤ The **BIG** Smoke.

›› Smokey

Born in Antigua, the cricketer Viv Richards (b.1952) made
his debut for the West Indies in 1974, captaining the team
from 1985 to 1991. During his Test career Richards scored
over 6,000 runs. He was nicknamed **Smokey** because of his
resemblance to the boxer **Smokin' Joe** Frazier.

›› Smokin' Joe

Joe Frazier (b.1944) was world heavyweight champion
1970–73. The non-stop fiery aggression with which he threw
his left hooks earned Frazier his nickname **Smokin' Joe**. He
fought Muhammad Ali in the famous 'Thrilla in Manila' in
1975.

›› Smudger

Smudger (or **Smudge**) is a nickname commonly attached to the surname Smith. This probably stems from the idea of a blacksmith's face being blackened with dirty marks from the smoke.

›› Sniffer

Footballer Allan Clarke (b.1946) played for Leeds United 1969–78 and won 19 caps for England. He was known as **Sniffer** because of his ability to sniff out goal-scoring opportunities.

›› Snowy

The nickname **Snowy** is traditionally attached to the surname Baker, especially by Australians, from the idea that a baker is always covered in white flour. The most famous Australian so-named was Reginald 'Snowy' Baker (1884–1953), an all-round sportsman who excelled in many sports including boxing, rugby union, swimming, and water polo.

›› Son of Sam

David Berkowitz (b.1953) terrorized New York City from July 1976 to August 1977, killing six young women in attacks on courting couples before he was caught. Berkowitz called himself **Son of Sam** in letters he wrote to the press and the police department, a name he took from that of his neighbour Sam Carr.

›› The Sooner State

Oklahoma is popularly known as the **Sooner State**. *Sooner* here is in the sense 'one who acts prematurely', referring to those who tried to get into the frontier territory of Oklahoma before the US government formally opened it to settlers in 1889. Oklahoma City was settled virtually overnight in a land rush. A Sooner is colloquially a native of Oklahoma.

❯❯ Spaghetti Junction

Spaghetti Junction is the informal name for Gravelly Hill interchange on the M6 near Birmingham in the UK, opened in 1971. The term *spaghetti junction* can be applied to any similarly complex multi-level junction of intersecting roads, especially one on a motorway.

❯❯ Sparky

In the 1980s and 1990s, Welsh footballer Mark Hughes (b.1962) made 345 league appearances for Manchester United and 108 for Chelsea, also playing for such clubs as Barcelona, Bayern Munich, and Southampton. Hughes was known as **Sparky** because of his fiery, combative temperament on the pitch. He has gone on to manage the Welsh national team.

❯❯ The Speck

The island of Tasmania is sometimes referred to by the derogatory nickname the **Speck** on account of its tiny size compared to continental Australia.

❯❯ The Sphinx

After Franklin D. Roosevelt (1882–1945) had served two terms as US president, his inscrutability in 1939 regarding his intentions about seeking a third term led the press to refer to him as the **Sphinx**.

❯❯ Spider[1]

The nickname **Spider** is traditionally associated with the surnames Webb and Kelly. 'Spider' Webb is an almost inevitable pun. 'Spider' Kelly comes from the Irish boxer Jimmy 'Spider' Kelly, who won the British and Empire featherweight title in 1938, and his son Billy 'Spider' Kelly (b.1932) who took the same title in 1955.

›› Spider²

The US tennis player Althea Gibson (1927–2003) was the
first black player to win a major singles title. Gibson's titles
included the French and Italian championships (1956) and
the British and American titles (1957 and 1958). She was
nicknamed **Spider** because of her long legs and spider-like
scurrying at the net.

›› Spike

In the army and navy the nickname **Spike** has long been
associated with the surname Sullivan. This probably derives
from William 'Spike' Sullivan, a boxer at the turn of the 20th
century. There are a number of famous show-business Spikes.
The 1950s US comic bandleader Spike Jones (1911–65) was
born Lindley Armstrong Jones. The son of a railroad worker,
he was said to be as skinny as a railroad spike, hence his
childhood nickname. Spike Milligan (1918–2002), the
comedian and author, was born Terence Milligan to Irish
parents in India. As a young man he was a promising jazz
musician and took the name Spike, either after Spike Jones
or perhaps after the British jazz composer Spike Hughes. The
US film director Spike Lee (b. Shelton Jackson Lee, 1957)
was given his nickname by his mother because he was such a
tough child. In the TV series *Buffy the Vampire Slayer*, the
character of Spike is so-named because of the vampire's
former habit of torturing his victims with railroad spikes,
which brings us back to Spike Jones.

›› The Spireites

Chesterfield football club are known as the **Spireites** because
of the famous crooked spire of the town's St Mary's All Saints
Church.

›› The Splendid Splinter

US baseball player Ted Williams (b.1918) was known as the

Splendid Splinter because of his skinny frame and batting prowess. His other famous nickname was ····▶ TEDDY Ballgame.

▶▶ Spud

Spud is the inevitable nickname given to anyone with the surname Murphy. A spud is an informal term for a potato, traditionally a staple crop in Ireland. Murphy is a common Irish surname and itself a colloquial word for a potato.

▶▶ Spurs

In 1882 a group of London schoolboys formed a football team which they named Hotspur FC. The name came from Harry Hotspur, the Shakespearean character and member of the Northumberland family, whose ancestral home was near Tottenham Marshes where their first matches were played. A few years later the club's name was changed to Tottenham Hotspur. Its nickname **Spurs** is an abbreviation of *Hotspur*.

▶▶ The Square Mile

The City of London, the part of London governed by the Lord Mayor and the Corporation, is known as the **Square Mile**. An important commercial and financial centre, its precise area is 677 acres, slightly over one square mile.

▶▶ The Squatter State

Immediately before the Civil War, both pro-slavery and anti-slavery groups tried to rush settlers into the territory of Kansas, hence one of the state's nicknames the **Squatter State**.

▶▶ Squiffy

Herbert Henry Asquith (1852–1928), British Prime Minister 1908–16, had a reputation as a heavy drinker, which earned him his nickname **Squiffy** or **Old Squiffy**. After he had been displaced as Prime Minister by Lloyd George in December 1916, his followers became known as 'Squiffites'.

›› Stan the Man

Who **Stan the Man** is depends on whether you are American or British. To Americans the nickname applies to the baseball player Stan Musial (b.1920). One of the most consistent performers in the history of the game, he played his entire career with the St Louis Cardinals (1941–63). In British sport, the nickname belongs to the English footballer Stan Collymore (b.1971), whose clubs included Crystal Palace, Nottingham Forest, Liverpool, and Aston Villa.

›› Steel Magnolia

Rosalynn Carter (b.1927), wife of President Jimmy Carter, was US First Lady 1977–81. The term 'steel magnolia' is used in the US to describe a woman from the southern states who has a tough character beneath a feminine and seemingly fragile exterior. Together with **Iron Magnolia**, it was often applied to Rosalynn Carter.

›› Sticks

The English fashion model Twiggy was born Lesley Hornby (b.1949). She began her modelling career in 1966, becoming famous for her skinny boyish look. Her professional name was a nickname given to her by the photographer Justin de Villeneuve, and was itself based on her schoolgirl nickname of **Sticks**.

›› Stormin' Norman

Norman Schwarzkopf (b.1935) was Commander-in-Chief of the Allied forces during the Gulf War (1991). Early in his army career he was dubbed **Stormin' Norman** on account of his forceful personality and quick temper.

▶▶ Stroller

As a football player George Graham (b.1944) was a member
of the 1970–71 Arsenal side that won the League and Cup
double. He repeated this feat as a manager with the same
club in 1993. Graham was dubbed **Stroller** during his
playing days at Arsenal, because of his unhurried calm in
midfield.

▶▶ The Stub-toe State

One of the US state of Montana's early nicknames was the
Stub-toe State because of its steep mountain slopes.

▶▶ La Stupenda

The Australian operatic soprano Joan Sutherland (b.1926)
was acclaimed for her performance of the title role in
Donizetti's *Lucia di Lammermoor* at Covent Garden in 1959.
Following her Italian debut in the same role two years later,
the Milanese press gave her the title **La Stupenda**.

▶▶ The Sucker State

The US state of Illinois is known as the **Sucker State**, perhaps
from the fact that the local miners went to the mines in the
spring and returned in the autumn, just as the sucker fish did
in the rivers.

▶▶ Sugar

The boxer Sugar Ray Robinson (1920–89) was born Walker
Smith. He took the name Ray Robinson in 1940 when he
turned up for an amateur fight without registering with the
authorities and borrowed the card of another boxer,
afterwards deciding to keep his adopted name. On a later
occasion his manager George Gainford is said to have replied
to a reporter's remark that Robinson was a 'sweet' fighter,
'Yes, he's as sweet as sugar'. From then on the boxer was

known as Sugar Ray Robinson. Robinson was world welterweight champion 1946–51 and middleweight champion 1951–60. The *Sugar* tag was adopted by a later boxer Sugar Ray Leonard (b.1956).

›› The Sultan of Spin[1]

Peter Mandelson. See ····➤ The **PRINCE** of Darkness[2].

›› The Sultan of Spin[2]

Shane Warne. See ····➤ **HOLLYWOOD**.

›› The Sultan of Swat

Babe Ruth (1895–1948), the US baseball player, became known as the **Sultan of Swat** because of the force with which he hit (or 'swatted') the ball. The historical Sultan of Swat, or more properly the Akond of Swat, was Saidu Baba (d.1877), the ruler and high priest of Swat, a region of the northwestern part of the Indian subcontinent. The Akond of Swat was the subject of a piece of nonsense verse by the poet Edward Lear in 1873.

›› The Sunflower State

The **Sunflower State** is Kansas. The sunflower is the state flower of Kansas, where they grow abundantly.

›› Sunny Jim

James Callaghan (b.1912), British Prime Minister 1976–79, was noted for his cheery disposition and so widely known as **Sunny Jim**, a name which can be applied to any cheerful person. It comes from the name of a character used to advertise Force breakfast cereal early in the 20th century: 'High o'er the fence leaps Sunny Jim/'Force' is the food that raises him.'

›› The Sunshine State

The nickname the **Sunshine State** is most closely associated with Florida, famous for its hot climate. It has also been applied to New Mexico, South Dakota, and California.

›› Superbrat

John McEnroe (b.1959) dominated men's tennis in the early 1980s. Among his many titles are three Wimbledon singles titles (1981, 1983–84) and four US Open singles championships (1979–81, 1984). Nicknamed **Superbrat** and **Mac the Mouth** by the press, he was a temperamental player with a fiery temper on court, his outbursts often directed against the umpire or line judges. McEnroe was regularly fined for his tantrums and at the Australian Open in 1990 he was disqualified from the tournament for verbally abusing officials.

›› Supermac[1]

The *London Evening Standard* cartoonist Vicky (Victor Weisz (1913–66)) first depicted the prime minister Harold Macmillan (1894–1986) as **Supermac** on 6 November 1958. He caricatured Macmillan as an elderly Superman, the US comic strip character. The nickname, intended to be mockingly satirical, came to be used instead as a term of admiration and affection.

›› Supermac[2]

Malcolm Macdonald (b.1950), the English footballer, was a star player for Newcastle United in the 1970s. Known as **Supermac** by the fans, Macdonald won 14 international caps, scoring five goals for England against Cyprus on 16 April 1975.

›› Supermex

The golfer Lee Trevino (b.1939) was born in Dallas, Texas, of Mexican parentage. He won three of the Majors twice: the US

Open (1968, 1971), the British Open (1971, 1972), and the PGA (1974, 1984). Famous for his wise-cracking exuberance on the course, he was popularly known as **Supermex**.

▶▶ The Supremo

Louis Mountbatten, 1st Earl Mountbatten of Burma (1900–79) served in the Royal Navy before rising to become Supreme Allied Commander in South-East Asia (1943–45), hence his nickname the **Supremo**. As the last viceroy (1947) and first Governor-General of India (1947–48), he oversaw the independence of India and Pakistan.

▶▶ The Sweater Girl

The Hollywood actress Lana Turner (1920–95) was promoted as the **Sweater Girl** at the start of her career, when she was encouraged to wear tight-fitting sweaters to draw attention to her bust. Her films include *The Postman Always Rings Twice* (1946), *The Bad and the Beautiful* (1952), and *Imitation of Life* (1959).

▶▶ Swee' Pea

Billy Strayhorn (1915–67) was a jazz pianist who worked closely with Duke Ellington as an arranger and composer. Among his compositions is 'Take the "A" Train', which became Ellington's signature tune. It was Ellington who gave his young collaborator the nickname **Swee' Pea**, naming him after the hyperactive baby in the Popeye comic strip cartoon.

Surnames

Certain nicknames inevitably attach themselves to particular
surnames, especially among members of the armed forces.
Most of those listed below are entries in this dictionary, where
their origins are explained:

Blacky White
Blanco White
Chalky White
Bunny Austin or Austen or Warren
Buster Crabbe
Daisy Bell or May
Dickie Bird
Ding-Dong Bell
Dinty Moore
Dixie Dean
Dusty Miller or Rhodes
Dutchy Holland
Johnnie Walker
Lefty Wright
Muddy Waters
Nobby Clark or Clarke
Pincher Martin
Rusty Steele
Sandy Brown
Shiner Bright
Smudger Smith
Snowy Baker
Spider Kelly or Webb
Spike Sullivan
Spud Murphy
Tod Hunter or Sloan
Tommy Atkins
Tug Wilson

>> Sweetness

The American footballer Walter Payton (1954–99) joined the
Chicago Bears as a running back in 1975, spending his entire
career with them until he retired in 1987. At the end of his
13-year career, he had set an NFL rushing record of 16,726
yds (finally broken in 2002 by Emmitt Smith). Payton was
known as **Sweetness**, a nickname from his days playing for
Jackson State University, both for the smoothness of his
running style and for his temperament.

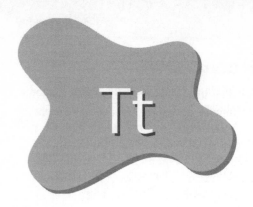

Tall

Tall people can find themselves given such nicknames as **Lofty**, **Spider**, **Stretch**, and the ironic alternatives **Shorty**, **Titch**, **Tiny**, and **Tiny Tim**. Strangely Tiny is more often used as a nickname for a tall man than a short one, in the same way that Robin Hood's towering companion was dubbed Little John. The same kind of perverse humour accounts for Lofty being applied to short people.

History gives us such examples of height-related nicknames as **Longshanks** (Edward I) and **Long Tom** (Thomas Jefferson). Nicknames of famously tall people who appear in this book include the **Ambling Alp** (Primo Carnera); **Big Bill** (Bill Tilden); **Big Bird** (Joel Garner); **Big Train** (Walter Johnson); the **Long Fellow** (both Eamon de Valera and Lester Piggott); **Wilt the Stilt** (Wilt Chamberlain).

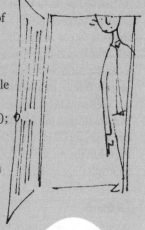

❯❯ The Tar Heel State

Why is the US state of North Carolina known as the **Tar Heel State**? This unusual nickname comes from Tarheel, a term for a person from North Carolina dating from the middle of the 19th century. During a battle in the Civil War a brigade of North Carolinians failed to hold a position. Soldiers from Mississippi mockingly told them that if they had only tarred their heels that morning, they would have stuck to the ground better.

❯❯ The Tart with the Cart

On Dublin's Grafton St is a statue of Molly Malone, the seafood-seller famous from the old Dublin song in which she sings 'Cockles and mussels, alive, alive, oh!' Locals refer to the statue of Molly, depicted in a low-cut dress and pushing a handcart, as the **Tart with the Cart**.

❯❯ Tarzan

In the late 1980s and 1990s, Michael Heseltine (b.1933), the British Conservative politician, was known in the popular press as **Tarzan** and he was often pictured in cartoons wearing a loin cloth. The nickname was coined by the Labour MP Stanley Clinton-Davis because he thought that Heseltine looked a bit like Johnny Weissmuller, an actor who had played Tarzan in a series of films. In fact Clinton-Davis had got Weissmuller confused with Lex Barker, another screen Tarzan altogether. But with his mane of blond hair and dynamic, virile image, Heseltine suited the nickname and it soon caught on. His autobiography, published in 2000, was appropriately titled *Life in the Jungle*.

❯❯ Tassie

Tasmania is sometimes known as **Tassie** for short.

❯❯ Teddy Ballgame

The US baseball player Ted Williams (1918–2002) played for

19 years with the Boston Red Sox (1939–60), during which he had 2,654 hits and hit 521 home runs. His nickname **Teddy Ballgame** reflects his standing as one of the all-time baseball greats.

❯❯ The Teflon Don

In the 1980s and 90s, John Gotti (1940–2002), the US Mafia boss, was known by the New York tabloids as the **Teflon Don**. This was because none of the charges brought against him in three criminal trials could be made to 'stick' and he was acquitted each time.

Margaret Thatcher

Margaret Thatcher was given many nicknames, some complimentary, some disapproving, and some descriptive. Perhaps the most famous one was the **Iron Lady**, which seemed to sum up so well her steely, unyielding determination. During her time as prime minister, **Maggie** was the most common nickname used in the British popular press, especially in headlines. Other nicknames for Margaret Thatcher include:

Attila the Hen — pun on Attila the Hun
Blessed Margaret — as with The **Leaderene**, an ironic compliment, both coined by Norman St John Stevas
The Grocer's Daughter — literally true, but also because she followed as Tory PM 'Grocer' Heath
The Milk Snatcher — abolished free school milk when Minister of Education
The Mummy — jokey reference by Thatcher herself to the film poster 'The Mummy Returns'
Tina — from 'There Is No Alternative'

›› The Teflon President

Ronald Reagan (1911–2004), President of the US 1981–89,
seemed able to shrug off all sorts of blunders and scandals
during his presidency without his reputation being unduly
tarnished. Nothing appeared to stick to Reagan, hence the
label that became attached to him: the **Teflon President**. In
1983 Patricia Shroeder said in a speech made in the US
House of Representatives: 'Ronald Reagan…is attempting a
great breakthrough in political technology—he has been
perfecting the Teflon-coated Presidency. He sees to it that
nothing sticks to him.'

›› The Teflon Terminator

Arnold Schwarzenegger. See ····➤ The **GOVERNOR**.

›› The Thief of Badgags

Milton Berle (1908–2002) was an enormous star of US
television in the 1950s. One of his nicknames was the **Thief
of Badgags**, playing on the title of the film *The Thief of
Baghdad* (1940). He was best known, though, as
····➤ **MR** Television.

›› The Thinking Man's Crumpet

Joan Bakewell (b.1933) is a British broadcaster who in the
late 1960s presented the arts magazine programme *Late
Night Line-Up*. Intelligent and attractive, she was dubbed the
Thinking Man's Crumpet by the humorist Frank Muir. The
term has since been applied to a succession of women
including Gillian Anderson, Nigella Lawson, and Carol
Vorderman. When Anderson heard she had been so
described, she apparently replied 'Well, it's more flattering
than being a lobotomized man's crumpet, I suppose'. Men
who have attracted the label **Thinking Woman's Crumpet**
include Michael Palin, Michael Ignatieff, Colin Firth, and
George Clooney.

Thin

Common nicknames for a skinny person include **Beanpole**, **Lanky**, **Slim**, and **Stick Insect**. A good historical example is Pitt the Younger, who was known as the **Bottomless Pitt**. Nicknames in this book prompted by an individual's thinness include **Bones** (Frank Sinatra); the **Shrimp** (Jean Shrimpton); and the **Splendid Splinter** (Ted Williams). As a teenager, the tennis player Ken Rosewall was so skinny that he was ironically dubbed **Muscles**. Lesley Hornby is better known as the 1960s fashion model **Twiggy**, a professional name that was originally a nickname. As a schoolgirl she was known as **Sticks**.

➤➤ The Thorpedo

The Australian swimmer Ian Thorpe (b.1982) is the dominant figure in world swimming at the start of the new millennium. He won three gold medals at the 2000 Olympic Games, six golds in the 2002 Commonwealth Games, and has broken numerous world records. Thorpe's nickname is a pun on his surname and the word *torpedo*, suggesting his speed in the water. In Australia he is generally known simply as **Thorpey**. He famously has a shoe size of 17.

➤➤ Three-Fingered Brown

Mordecai Brown (1876–1948) was a US baseball pitcher in the early 1900s. When he was a boy he lost half the index finger of his right hand, and had his small finger paralysed, in a farming accident. Known as **Three-Fingered Brown**, he learned to use the stump of the missing finger to give extra spin to his curve ball.

➤➤ The Throstles

The official nickname of West Bromwich Albion football club is the **Throstles** because of the thrushes, or throstles (a Black Country word), that used to be seen around the hedges in the Hawthorns area of West Bromwich. In 1900 the club moved here to a new ground which was named The Hawthorns. The club's fans prefer the nickname
····➤ the **BAGGIES**.

➤➤ Thumper

In the early days of Tony Blair's leadership of the Labour Party, deputy leader John Prescott (b.1938) was portrayed as **Thumper** to Blair's Bambi. In the Disney cartoon film *Bambi* (1942), based on Felix Salten's story for children (1923), the rabbit Thumper is the young deer Bambi's best friend. The nickname fitted well with Prescott's image as one of the 'bruisers' of British politics. Newspaper cartoons at the time pictured the pair as the Disney characters.

➤➤ The Thunderer

One of the most famous newspaper nicknames is the **Thunderer**. Originally this was a title given to Edward Sterling (1773–1847), who contributed columns to *The Times* newspaper and later became its assistant editor. It is probably a reference to one of his leading articles in 1829, in which he wrote: 'We thundered forth the other day an article on social and political reform'. By the middle of the 19th century the nickname had transferred to *The Times* itself.

›› Tich

An alternative spelling of ····➤ TITCH.

›› The Tiger

Georges Clemenceau (1841–1929) was Prime Minister of
France 1906–9 and 1917–20. He negotiated the Treaty of
Versailles in 1919. Clemenceau was known as the **Tiger**
because of his tigerish determination and stubbornness.

›› The Tigers

Hull City football club's nickname the **Tigers** derives from the
team's amber and black strip.

›› Tiger Tim

Will it be *Tiger Tim roars to victory* or *Tiger Tim tamed*? Every
summer, during the two weeks of the Wimbledon tennis
tournament, the British tabloids are full of headlines
featuring **Tiger Tim**, the nickname of the tennis player Tim
Henman (b.1974), on whom most British hopes for a
Wimbledon singles champion have been pinned in recent
years. Although presumably intended to suggest gutsy
aggression, the name does sit slightly awkwardly with
Henman's easygoing temperament. The original Tiger Tim
was a cartoon character, leader of a group of animals known
as the Bruin Boys, who first appeared in the *Daily Mirror* in
1904, and later in the *Rainbow* comic (1914–56).

›› Tina

Margaret Thatcher (b.1925) was British Prime Minister
1979–90. She was sometimes known as **Tina**, from the initial
letters of the phrase *There Is No Alternative*. The phrase
originally came from a speech Thatcher made to the
Conservative Women's Conference, 21 May 1980, when she
asserted, in reference to the necessity of tough economic
measures, 'I believe people accept there is no alternative'.

▶▶ The Tinkerman

Claudio Ranieri (b.1951) was the manager of Chelsea
football club 2000–04. In 2003 the Russian billionaire
tycoon Roman Abramovich bought the club and made it
possible for Ranieri to build a large squad of star players by
spending huge sums of money on the transfer market.
Ranieri was known for making frequent changes to his team's
line-up, formation, and tactics, and was dubbed the
Tinkerman by the British press, a nickname the Italian
appeared to revel in.

▶▶ Tin Pan Alley

Tin Pan Alley was the nickname of a district in New York
(28th Street, between 5th Avenue and Broadway) where
many songwriters, arrangers, and publishers of popular
music were formerly based. Between the late 1880s and the
mid 20th century the term was synonymous with the
American popular music industry. In London, the name was
popularly applied to Denmark Street, off Charing Cross Road,
where music publishers, recording studios, and musical
instrument dealers congregated.

▶▶ Tiny

Some nicknames are deliberately ironic. Calling a very large
or tall person **Tiny** is like calling a bald man Curly or (in
Australia) a red-headed person Bluey. One of the most
famous Tinies was Tiny Rowland (1917–98), the multi-
millionaire businessman and founder of the giant Lonrho
conglomerate. Born Roland Fuhrhop, he was said to have
been originally nicknamed Tiny by his Indian nanny because
of his small size, though he grew up to be six feet tall.

▶▶ Titch

The story of how the name **Titch** (or **Tich**) came to mean a
small person is a convoluted one. Sir Roger Tichborne, heir

to the valuable Tichborne estate in Hampshire, was presumed drowned in a shipwreck in 1854. Then in 1866 a man claiming to be the lost Sir Roger arrived in England. His claim was disputed and proved to be false, however, and the fraudster, in fact Wapping butcher Arthur Orton (1834–98), was subsequently tried and imprisoned for perjury. Little Tich was the stage name of the diminutive music-hall comedian Harry Relph (1868–1928). He had been given this nickname as a child because he was thought to resemble the portly Arthur Orton, the Tichborne Claimant. From the 1930s, the word *tich*, or more commonly *titch*, has been an informal word for anyone of small stature. From this we also get the adjective *titchy*, meaning 'very small'.

›› Tod

The nickname **Tod** is traditionally attached to the surname Hunter, from the surname Todhunter (meaning 'fox hunter', from *tod*, an old dialect word for a fox). Men with the surname Sloan also used to find themselves nicknamed Tod, after the famous US jockey Tod Sloan (1873–1933). The phrase *on one's tod*, meaning 'on one's own', comes from the rhyming slang *on one's Tod Sloan*.

›› The Toffees

Everton football club have from early on in their history been known as the **Toffees** or the **Toffeemen**. This is because there used to be a sweet shop called *Ye Anciente Everton Toffee House* opposite the ground. Before kick-off, the owner used to throw toffees to the crowd.

›› Tokyo Rose

During the Second World War the name **Tokyo Rose** was given by US servicemen to a number of women broadcasting Japanese propaganda on Tokyo Radio. The name is usually associated with one such woman in particular, Iva Ikuko Toguri D'Aquino (b.1916), a

Japanese-American. After the war D'Aquino was convicted of treason and spent six years in prison, but in 1977 she was pardoned by President Ford. The name Tokyo Rose was echoed during the Vietnam War in Jane Fonda's nickname ····➤ **HANOI** Jane.

❯❯ Tommy

A male British soldier with the surname Atkins traditionally finds himself nicknamed **Tommy**. This is because a 'Tommy Atkins' is an old term for a private soldier in the British army. It dates from the 19th century and comes from the use of that name on specimen forms that were issued to new recruits.

❯❯ Tom Terrific

The US baseball player Tom Seaver (b.1944) pitched for 20 years in the major leagues, mainly with the New York Mets and the Cincinatti Reds. The power and technique of his pitching earned him his nickname **Tom Terrific**.

❯❯ The Tonypandy Terror

Born in Tonypandy, Wales, Tommy Farr (1913–86) was British heavyweight boxing champion 1937–38. In 1937 he challenged Joe Louis for the heavyweight title, and in an epic contest took the champion the full distance of 15 rounds but lost on points.

❯❯ The Toothpick State

The US state of Arkansas takes its nickname the **Toothpick State** from the bowie knife, also sometimes called a 'toothpick knife'. Many of the state's early settlers carried this long hunting knife, named after the American frontiersman Jim Bowie (1796–1836). The state has also been known as the **Bowie State**.

›› The Torygraph

The Daily Telegraph newspaper is known as the **Torygraph** because of the paper's traditional support of the British Conservative (or Tory) Party.

›› The Toy Bulldog

The US boxer Mickey Walker (1901–81) was world welterweight champion 1922–26 and world middleweight champion 1926–31. He was known as the **Toy Bulldog** because of his small stature, his rugged looks, and his tenacity in the ring.

›› The Tractor Boys

Ipswich Town football club are affectionately known to their fans as the **Tractor Boys** because of Ipswich's location in rural East Anglia. The nickname provides ample opportunity for such newspaper headlines as *Tractors plough out a draw* and *Tractor Boys run over Foxes* (that is, defeat Leicester City).

›› Trane

The US jazz saxophonist John Coltrane (1926–67) was a leading figure of the jazz avante-garde in the 1960s. Before forming his own quartet in 1960, he played in groups led by Dizzy Gillespie and Miles Davis. It was while a member of the Miles Davis quintet that he was first nicknamed **Trane**, an abbreviation of his surname. One of his albums was called *The Last Trane*.

›› The Treasure State

The US state of Montana is noted for its gold, silver, copper, and coal mines, hence its official nickname the **Treasure State**.

➤➤ Tricky Dick

Richard Nixon (1913–94) was President of the US 1969–74
before the Watergate scandal forced him to resign. He was
called **Tricky Dick** (or **Tricky Dicky** in Britain) because of his
reputation for political trickery, cunning, and evasiveness.
The nickname was coined by Helen Gahagan Douglas, his
opponent in the 1950 senatorial election in California. Nixon
ran a dirty campaign in which he tried to smear the liberal
Douglas as a Communist sympathizer, labelling her the **Pink
Lady**. Nixon's nickname later came to the fore during the
investigation into his involvement in the Watergate
conspiracy during his 1972 re-election campaign and its
attempted cover-up.

➤➤ Tug

Tug is the traditional nickname in the British armed forces,
particularly the Royal Navy, for a man with the surname
Wilson. It appears to derive from Admiral Sir Arthur Knyvet
Wilson (1842–1921) whose nickname was 'Tug' Wilson. This
followed an incident in which he ordered a battleship to
enter harbour and, when it repeatedly had difficulties in
doing so, offered in exasperation to have it towed into port
with tugs.

➤➤ Tugga

The Australian cricketer Steve Waugh (b.1965) made his Test
debut in 1985–86 and was captain of Australia from 1999 to
2004. His nickname **Tugga** Waugh (a pun on 'tug-of-war')
suits his tough, fiercely competitive personality. His twin
brother Mark is known as ····➤ AFGHAN.

➤➤ Twiggy

Lesley Hornby. See ····➤ STICKS.

›› Two Brains

The British Conservative MP David Willetts (b.1956) rejoices in the nickname **Two Brains**, referring to his reputation as an intellectual and a policy expert. It was coined by *The Guardian* journalist Michael White. In 1996 Willetts was forced to resign as Paymaster General following a report by the House of Commons Standards and Privileges Committee which accused him of 'dissembling' during the course of a select committee investigation. A cartoon at the time wittily alluded to his nickname, depicting Willetts's desk empty except for a bottle of whisky and two revolvers.

›› Two Dinners

The top British lawyer Arnold Goodman (1914–95) played a large part in British legal and political life in the 1960s, acting as legal adviser to the prime ministers Harold Wilson and Edward Heath. Lord Goodman's girth and healthy appetite earned him the nickname **Two Dinners**. Later nicknames modelled on this one include ····➤ TWO BRAINS and ····➤ TWO JAGS.

›› Two-Gun Patton

In the Second World War, General George Smith Patton (1885–1945) commanded the 7th Army during the Sicilian campaign (1943) and the 3rd Army in the Normandy invasion (1944), advancing rapidly across France and into Germany. A larger-than-life character, he always wore two pearl-handled revolvers, hence his nickname **Two-Gun Patton**.

›› Two Jags

At the Labour Party conference in 1999, John Prescott (b.1938), then responsible for the transport portfolio as well as being deputy prime minister, used two cars to make the 300-yard journey from his hotel to the conference centre in order to deliver a speech urging less car use. This prompted William Hague, leader of the Conservative Party, to remark: 'People work hard and save hard to own a car. They do not want to be told that they cannot drive it by a Deputy Prime Minister whose idea of a park and ride scheme is to park one Jaguar and drive away in another.' On 16 May 2001, during the General Election campaign, Prescott punched egg-throwing protester Craig Evans in Rhyl. His nickname **Two Jags** was neatly converted to **Two Jabs** on the front page of the following morning's *Sun* newspaper. The paper's leading article was headlined 'Thrilla in Rhyla', echoing the 'Thrilla in Manila' heavyweight-title fight between Muhammad Ali and Joe Frazier in 1975.

❯❯ Two-Ton Tessie

The British variety artist Tessie O'Shea (1917–95) was a bubbly ukulele-playing performer whose nickname **Two-Ton Tessie** came from her size and her song 'Two-Ton Tessie from Tennessee'. In 1945 the RAF nicknamed a 22,000 lb bomb 'Ten-Ton Tessie' after her.

›› The Unabomber

The **Unabomber** was a media nickname for a terrorist who carried out a series of bomb attacks in the US between 1978 and 1995 as part of an anarchist, anti-technology personal crusade. Because the attacks were made on academic institutions (and particularly scientists), the name Unabomber, a blend of *university* and *bomber*, was coined. Theodore Kaczynski (b.1942), a former mathematics teacher at Berkeley University, was finally arrested and charged in 1996. In 1998 he was sentenced to four life terms of imprisonment.

›› Uncle Joe

Uncle Joe was a British wartime nickname for Joseph Stalin (1879–1953) as the personification of Soviet Russia. The name is first recorded in a comment made by Winston Churchill to Franklin Roosevelt in 1943: 'The castigation we have both received from Uncle Joe...was naturally to be expected'.

›› Uncle Miltie

Milton Berle. See ····▶ MR Saturday Night.

›› The Uncle of Europe

Edward VII (1841–1910) was known as the **Uncle of Europe**, which was literally true. Edward was uncle to the German

Kaiser, the Queen of Spain, and the Queen of Norway. Not only that, but his wife Queen Alexandra was aunt to the Tsar of Russia, the King of Denmark, and the King of Greece. His mother Queen Victoria had been known as the **Grandmother of Europe**.

›› The Unknown Prime Minister

In 1922 Andrew Bonar Law (1858–1923) succeeded Lloyd George as British Prime Minister, but died unexpectedly after only a year in office. He was buried in Westminster Abbey and his predecessor Herbert Asquith commented 'It is fitting that we should have buried the Unknown Prime Minister by the side of the Unknown Soldier.'

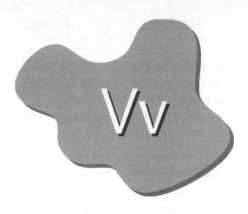

▶▶ The Valentine State

The US state of Arizona was admitted into the Union on 14 February (St Valentine's Day) 1912, hence its nickname the **Valentine State**. Until Alaska was admitted in 1959, Arizona was also known as the **Baby State**.

▶▶ Van the Man

To his admirers Van Morrison (b.1945) is simply **Van the Man**. The Belfast-born rock singer-songwriter has produced many albums including *Astral Weeks* (1968), *Moondance* (1970), and *Down the Road* (2002). His style blends jazz, blues, R&B, and folk.

▶▶ The Velvet Fog

The US singer Mel Tormé (1925–99) was greatly admired for his smooth crooning style. He formed his own group the Mel-Tones in the 1940s, during which time he became known as the **Velvet Fog**, and in the second half of the decade he went solo. His autobiography was entitled *It Wasn't All Velvet*.

▶▶ The Venice of the North

The Dutch city of Amsterdam is built, like Venice, on numerous islands separated by canals and connected by bridges, hence its nickname the **Venice of the North**. The title

is also claimed by Stockholm in Sweden. Other 'Venices' are
the cities of Bangkok, Thailand (the **Venice of the East**) and
Glasgow, Scotland (the **Venice of the West**).

>> Vinegar Joe

Joseph W. Stilwell (1883–1946) acquired his army nickname
Vinegar Joe when serving at the Infantry School, Fort Benning,
Georgia (1929–33), because of his acid tongue. During the
Second World War, Stilwell commanded Chiang Kai-shek's
troops in Burma, when his caustic and irascible manner was
evident in his dealings with other military leaders.

>> The Voice

In the 1940s Frank Sinatra (1915–98) was promoted as 'The
Voice that Thrills Millions', soon shortened to the **Voice**. The
tag was coined either by the singer's press agent George
Evans or by his agent Harry Kilby. It was the title of one his
earliest albums (1945).

>> The Voice of London

John Snagge (1904–96) began his career as a BBC radio
announcer in 1928. During the Second World War, he
became known as the **Voice of London**, authoritatively
announcing such momentous events as the D-Day landings,
VE Day, and VJ Day. He commentated on every Oxford-
Cambridge Boat Race between 1931 and 1980.

>> The Volunteer State

Tennessee's official nickname the **Volunteer State** comes
from the large number of volunteers (some 30,000 men)
contributed by Tennessee to the Mexican War of 1847.

>> The Vulcan

The British Conservative politician John Redwood (b.1951)
was secretary of state for Wales 1993–95. In the mid 1990s

newspapers called him the **Vulcan**, after the race of aliens to which Mr Spock belongs in the *Star Trek* science fiction series. Vulcans are noted for their logic, lack of emotion, and mental prowess, all characteristics that the politician was thought to share.

>> The Vulture

Emilio Butragueño (b.1963), the Spanish footballer, played for Real Madrid in the 1980s and 1990s and represented Spain 69 times, scoring 26 goals. His nickname **El Buitre** ('the Vulture' in Spanish) came partly from the similarity between his surname and the Spanish word for the bird of prey and partly from his predatory poaching of goals around the penalty area.

›› Wacko

Michael Jackson. See ····➤ JACKO.

›› The Walrus

Golf's **Walrus** is American Craig Stadler (b.1953), winner of the 1982 Masters. His thick, drooping moustache is thought to resemble the whiskers of a walrus, hence his nickname. He titled his autobiography *I am the Walrus*, after the Beatles song.

›› The Walrus of Love

Barry White (1944–2003) was aptly called the **Walrus of Love** because of his large frame, his deep growl of a voice, and his singing of sensual love ballads such as 'You're the First, the Last, My Everything' (1974) and 'Can't Get Enough of Your Love, Babe' (1974). In 2002, marine scientists at Birmingham's National Sea Life Centre were reported to have played Barry White songs to their sharks in an effort to get them to mate.

›› Wee Willie

Willie Keeler. See ····➤ HIT 'em Where They Ain't.

›› The Welsh Windbag

Neil Kinnock (b.1942) led the British Labour Party from 1983 to 1992. Born in Wales, he was a passionate but sometimes verbose speaker, attracting the disparaging nickname the **Welsh Windbag**.

▶▶ The Welsh Wizard[1]

David Lloyd George (1863–1945), British Prime Minister 1916–22, represented his Welsh constituency as an MP for 55 years. Lloyd George was known as the **Welsh Wizard** because of his masterly political skill and fiery oratory. John Maynard Keynes described him as, 'This extraordinary figure of our time, this syren, this goat-footed bard, this half-human visitor to our age from the hag-ridden magic and enchanted woods of Celtic antiquity'.

▶▶ The Welsh Wizard[2]

The Welsh footballer Billy Meredith (1874–1958) was an outstanding winger who during his long career played for both Manchester City and Manchester United and won 48 caps for Wales. He finally retired as a player at the age of 49.

▶▶ The Whirlwind

Snooker player Jimmy White (b.1962) earned the nickname the **Whirlwind** from his flamboyant, rapid-fire style of play. White has played in the final of the World Professional Championship six times but has been runner-up each time.

▶▶ Whispering Bob

Bob Harris (b.1946) presented the BBC TV music programme *The Old Grey Whistle Test* in the 1970s and became known as **Whispering Bob** because of his quietly spoken and laid-back style.

▶▶ Whispering Death

West Indian cricketer Michael Holding (b.1954) was an outstanding fast bowler. He was noted for his smooth, light-footed run-up, with which he could generate prodigious pace and fearsome bounce. His intimidating nickname **Whispering Death** stemmed from the fact that umpires used to claim that they couldn't hear him approaching behind them.

›› Whispering Grass

For nearly 30 years Shaw Taylor (b.1924) presented *Police Five* (1962–90), a weekly British TV programme in which the police sought the public's help in solving crimes. At the end of the programme he would remind viewers to 'keep 'em peeled'. Criminals are said to have referred to him as **Whispering Grass**, the title of a popular song written by Fred and Doris Fisher. 'Grass' is a slang term for a police informer.

›› The White Feather

The Italian footballer Fabrizio Ravanelli (b.1968) is known as the **White Feather** because of his prematurely grey hair. His clubs have included Perugia, Juventus, Middlesbrough, and Marseille.

›› White Lightning[1]

In 1976 the 6ft 2ins (188cm), long-striding Alberto Juantorena (b.1950) won Olympic gold medals at both the 400m and the 800m. His all-white running strip led the Cuban athlete to be known as **White Lightning**.

›› White Lightning[2]

Cricket's **White Lightning** was fast bowler Allan Donald (b.1966), the only bowler to take more than 300 Test wickets for South Africa. He was so called because of the exceptional speed of his bowling and his blond hair.

›› The White Shark

Greg Norman. See ····➤ The **GREAT** White Shark.

➤➤ The Wickedest Man in the World

Aleister Crowley. See ····➤ **BEAST** 666.

➤➤ Wilko

Jonny Wilkinson. See ····➤ **BOY** Bonkers.

➤➤ Wilt the Stilt

In his 14-year career playing basketball with the Philadelphia
Warriors, the Philadelphia 76ers and the Los Angeles Lakers,
Wilt Chamberlain (1936–99) dominated the sport in the
1960s and early 1970s. At 7ft 1in (216cm) he was known as
Wilt the Stilt, a nickname Chamberlain himself disliked. He
set many records, including averaging 50.4 in the 1961–62
season and once scoring 100 points in a game. Chamberlain
was also known as the **Big Dipper**, because he had to dip his
head as he walked through doorways.

➤➤ The Windy City

Chicago's well-known nickname the **Windy City**, while often
taken as a literal reference to the breezes of Lake Michigan, is
thought to have originally referred to its windbag politicians.
Recorded from the late 19th century, the tag was probably
coined by the *New York Sun* newspaper editor Charles A.
Dana.

➤➤ Winnie

Winston Churchill (1874–1965), British Prime Minister
1940–45 and 1951–55, was the inspirational leader of a
coalition government during the Second World War. The
familiar nickname **Winnie** reflects the great affection in
which Churchill was held by the British people.

➤➤ Wislon

Harold Wilson (1916–95) was British Prime Minister

1964–70 and 1974–76. Wilson was known to readers of the satirical magazine *Private Eye* as **Wislon**, a supposed (but recurrent) typographical error.

❯❯ The Wizard of Menlo Park

US inventor Thomas Edison (1847–1931) held more than a thousand patents for his inventions. Among these were the carbon microphone for telephones, the phonograph, and the carbon filament lamp. Edison also devised systems for generating and distributing electricity. He was known as the **Wizard of Menlo Park**, after the town in New Jersey where he lived and worked.

❯❯ The Wizard of Oz

Ozzie Smith (b.1954), one of the finest shortstops in baseball, played for the San Diego Padres and the St Louis Cardinals. His nickname the **Wizard of Oz** comes from his first name and is inspired by the character created by L. Frank Baum in his children's book *The Wonderful Wizard of Oz* (1900).

❯❯ The Wizard of the Dribble

In a football career that lasted until he was 50, Stanley Matthews (b.1915) played on the right wing for Stoke City and Blackpool and played for England 54 times. His outstanding performance for Blackpool in the 1953 FA Cup final meant that the match would be known ever after as the 'Matthews Final'. Matthews, the **Wizard of the Dribble**, was famous for his outstanding ball control, dancing down the right wing as he evaded opposing players. He was the first European Footballer of the Year in 1956 and was the first English footballer to be knighted.

❯❯ The Wolverine State

The **Wolverine State** is the US state of Michigan, where wolverines are found. A wolverine is a heavily-built carnivorous mammal, related to the weasel and noted for its strength and ferocity. The term has been used as a nickname for a native or inhabitant of Michigan since at least the 1830s.

▶▶ Woodbine Willie

Woodbine Willie was the nickname of Geoffrey Anketell Studdert Kennedy (1883–1929), the English priest and poet who served as a chaplain during the First World War, handing out Woodbine cigarettes to the soldiers in the trenches. Kennedy once described his ministry as taking 'a box of fags in your haversack and a great deal of love in your heart'.

▶▶ Wor Jackie

The English footballer Jackie Milburn (1924–88), a former pit apprentice, joined Newcastle United in 1943, going on to make 354 league appearances for the club and scoring 179 goals. Milburn was known to the adoring Newcastle fans as **Wor Jackie**, 'Wor' being a North-East English form of 'Our'. There is a bronze statue of him in the city centre.

▶▶ The World's Greatest Entertainer

Al Jolson (1886–1950) was the outstanding US entertainer of the 1920s and mid 1930s. He sang such hits as 'Swanee', 'Mammy', and 'Sonny Boy' in black make-up in imitation of black minstrel singers, often kneeling on one knee with his arms outstretched. Jolson starred in the first full-length talking film *The Jazz Singer* (1927), by which time he was already billing himself as the **World's Greatest Entertainer**.

▶▶ The World's Sweetheart

Mary Pickford. See ····▶ **AMERICA'S** Sweetheart.

›› Worzel

When he was leader of the Labour Party in the early 1980s, Michael Foot (b.1913) was nicknamed **Worzel**, after Worzel Gummidge, a talking scarecrow with straw hair who is the central character of a series of children's books by Barbara Euphan Todd (d.1976), later televised. The nickname was first used in the satirical *Dear Bill* letters by Richard Ingram and John Wells, published in *Private Eye* magazine and purporting to record the thoughts of Denis Thatcher during his wife's tenure as Prime Minister. Foot's white hair and slightly dishevelled appearance were thought to make him resemble the scarecrow.

›› Wottle the Throttle

The US middle-distance runner Dave Wottle (b.1950), usually wearing a golf cap, used to hang back until the final stretch when with a burst of speed he would snatch victory on the line. He won the 800m gold medal in the 1972 Olympics in the last few strides with just such a late run. This trademark acceleration at the end of a race earned him the rhyming nickname **Wottle the Throttle**.

▶▶ The Yankee Clipper

Baseball player Joe DiMaggio (1914–99) was first dubbed
the **Yankee Clipper** around 1940, referring both to his team
the New York Yankees and to the speed with which he
dispatched the ball. The original Yankee Clipper was a type of
US merchant ship built in the 19th century.

▶▶ Yardbird

Charlie Parker. See ····▶ BIRD.

▶▶ The Yellowhammer State

The US state of Alabama is nicknamed the **Yellowhammer
State**, from the yellowish tinge of the home-dyed grey
uniforms worn by the Confederate soldiers during the Civil
War.

▶▶ Yifter the Shifter

Miruts Yifter (b.1938), the Ethiopian long-distance runner,
won the 5,000m and 10,000m gold medals at the Moscow
Olympics in 1980. He was known as **Yifter the Shifter** because
of his ability to put on a sudden spurt in the last lap of a race.

▶▶ Yogi

Lawrence Berra (b.1925) played baseball for the New York
Yankees from 1946 to 1965, later becoming the team's

manager. His nickname **Yogi** Berra puns on the name of the US cartoon character Yogi Bear, created by William Hanna and Joseph Barbera.

›› The Yorkshire Ripper

In the late 1970s Peter Sutcliffe (b.1946) murdered 13 women in northern England and the Midlands before being captured in January 1981. The press branded Sutcliffe the **Yorkshire Ripper** because, like the 19th-century murderer Jack the Ripper, he mutilated his victims' bodies.

›› You Beaut Country

You Beaut Country is Australia. The phrase was originally coined by the Australian artist John Olsen (b.1928) in 1961 to describe the country's landscape as depicted in his series of paintings 'Journey into You Beaut Country'. In Australian English the colloquial phrase *you beaut* is used to express admiration or praise.

›› Yvonne

Princess Margaret (1930–2002), Elizabeth II's sister, was nicknamed **Yvonne** in the satirical magazine *Private Eye*.

≫ Zizou

Zinedine Zidane (b.1972), the French footballer, is affectionately known as **Zizou**. He was a key member of France's World Cup-winning team in 1998, heading two goals against Brazil in the final, and also helped France to victory in the European championship in 2000. Zidane's clubs include Bordeaux (whose coach coined his nickname), Juventus, and Real Madrid. The Spanish media call the player **El Zid**.

≫ Zoot

Jazz tenor saxophonist Zoot Sims (1925–85) was born John Haley Sims. It was in his teens playing with Ken Baker's band in 1941 that Sims came by his nickname **Zoot**. As a joke Baker made up a nickname for each of the music stands and painted it on the front. Sims was playing behind the stand with the word 'Zoot' on it, and the name stuck. The saxophone-playing character Zoot from *The Muppet Show* was named after Sims.

Index

›› Football clubs

›› Television and radio

›› Tennis